The Shining Star

C O L L E C T I O N

24 Christmas Advent Stories & Recipes

by Karen F. Skirten

Merry Christmas Emily & Cole!
Shine On!

FriesenPress

Suite 300 - 990 Fort St
Victoria, BC, Canada, V8V 3K2
www.friesenpress.com

ISBN
978-1-4602-5869-9 (Hardcover)
978-1-4602-5870-5 (Paperback)
978-1-4602-5871-2 (eBook)

1. Cooking, Holiday
2. Juvenile Fiction, Holidays & Celebrations, Christmas & Advent
3. Juvenile Fiction, Short Stories

Distributed to the trade by The Ingram Book Company

Table of Contents

1. "First Advent"

The winter storm blew in from the west quite suddenly, shaking the glass window panes in the house. Four-year-old Raymond lay in his bed listening to the wind howl and thought that it even sounded cold outside. As he slowly stretched his arms and yawned, he remembered that because of the blizzard, his parents had decided to keep safe and not drive into town for Church that morning. He rubbed his eyes, blinked a few times and then threw back his fluffy, warm duvet. Raymond jammed his feet into his slippers, put on his housecoat and made his way downstairs. *Oh boy, a whole Sunday to play*, he thought to himself.

His Mom and Dad were sitting at the kitchen table drinking their coffee and reading the newspaper. His Mom opened her arms and Raymond jumped on her lap.

"There's our big boy! Are you ready for some breakfast? How does pancakes and bacon sound?" his Mom said.

"I love pink eggs, Mom. I can eat a WHOLE stack of them!" Raymond had trouble saying pancakes and it sounded more like pink eggs. His Mom kissed him on the cheek and got up to make their breakfast.

His Dad smiled and poured him a glass of orange juice asking, "Did you have a good sleep, Ray?" Raymond sipped his juice and nodded yes.

He watched his Dad get up from the table and flip the wall calendar to a new picture. It was a picture of Santa on his sleigh. After he laid out three placemats, Dad set the table for breakfast. Raymond stared at that picture on the calendar. In it, Santa and his reindeer were flying over the houses below and in the back of the sleigh was a giant red bag with toys sticking out. High above in the sky though was a beautiful star lighting Santa's way.

It did not take long before his Mom placed a plate in front of him with three pancakes and two strips of bacon. After his Dad said grace, he poured syrup from the big bottle himself and then dug into his stack. Raymond liked lots of syrup.

"These are so yummy, Mom," Raymond murmured between sticky bites.

When they were done eating, Raymond helped his Dad clear the table and put the dishes in the dishwasher. Then he and his Mom went upstairs to make the beds and get dressed for the day.

While he was brushing his teeth his Mom said, "Honey, today is a very special day. Today is the first of December and it is also the First Advent."

Raymond frowned and asked, "What does First Advent mean, Mom?"

"Well, today is the first of four Sundays before Christ's birthday on Christmas Day," she replied. "We will light one candle tonight and say a prayer of thanks to God for giving us the gift of his son Jesus. Next Sunday, we will light two candles and the Sunday after that three and on the final Sunday, we light all four candles."

"How come all the candles on my birthday cake are there all at once, Mom?" Raymond asked.

His Mom laughed and said, "Well, you are a very special boy, but Jesus was the MOST special child ever born so we celebrate the arrival of his birthday for four whole weeks. Now, why don't you play with your train set for a while and I will call you when I get everything set up in the kitchen? We are going to start the Christmas baking today since we can't go outside. I thought we would start with the Gingersnaps."

Raymond scampered off to play with his trains. Not long afterwards, his Mom called him to come downstairs.

"Ready to bake some Christmas magic, Son?" she asked.

"You bet!" he replied eagerly.

"Okay, what is the first thing we do before we cook anything?" she asked.

"I know, I know, Mom, we have to wash our hands," he sighed. Once he was all washed up and had on his special apron, his Mom pulled up a stool to the kitchen counter for him to stand on. On the counter she had laid out shortening, eggs, sugar, bottles of spice and the big flour container. There was also a yellow box that he had never seen before.

"What is that, Mom?" he asked.

"That is called molasses and it makes the cookies dark and sweet," she told him.

His Mom creamed the shortening in the big cookie baking bowl. Then she let him pour in the sugar and she creamed it all together. Next came the egg, spices and that black "mole" stuff. When she had that all mixed together, Raymond helped his Mom by pouring in the bowl of flour and all the other stuff she had ready.

"Okay, Ray, now the fun part." Working together they each took pieces of the dough and rolled them into balls in their hands. They felt cool and squishy. Once they were perfectly round he dropped them into a small bowl of sugar and tossed them in it with a fork until they were covered. His Mom then placed them onto cookie sheets and put them into the oven to bake. While they were working his Mom told him that this was always the first Christmas baking her Mother used to do too, and before that, Great Grandma did the same thing.

"That is quite a production line you two having going," his Dad said as he walked into the kitchen from his basement workshop.

"What is a production line, Dad?" Raymond asked.

"Well, it is where people come together and each take a piece of the work so that the job gets done quicker, Ray. Just like at Santa's workshop, each Elf has a job to do and when everyone does their own job, great things can get accomplished. Another word you can use instead of calling it a production line is teamwork," his Dad explained. "You know, Raymond, the month of December is a very busy month with lots of fun, special traditions that need to get done. Mommy and I will need you to help us get ready for the big day. I know you can be a good boy and help us both out, can't you?"

Soon, the wonderful smell of ginger cookies filled the house. When they came out of the oven to cool there were so many that Raymond could not count that high. His Mom then let him help her pack them into a cookie tin to put into the freezer until Christmas. She kept six cookies out. One for Raymond, one for his Dad and one for her to eat right away while they were still warm, and then three "for later", she said.

They spent the afternoon in the living room. Mom read her book and Dad helped him build a puzzle of a gingerbread house. His Dad found the four corner pieces and then Raymond filled in the rest of the pieces. After the puzzle was done Raymond helped his Mom with folding their clean laundry. He matched up all the socks for her to fold. Later in the day, his Dad started a fire in the fireplace while his Mom got dinner ready. After they ate their dinner and he had had his bath, Raymond came back downstairs to the living room. His Dad had turned off all but one light in the room, which added to the special glow the fireplace cast.

Together, they gathered around a special blue candle his Mom had placed in the middle of the fireplace mantle. She lit the candle and then they all held hands and prayed to God in thanks for the miracle that he gave the world; his son Jesus.

Before going up to bed Raymond and his parents cuddled up on the couch and they each ate another Gingersnap cookie with a glass of milk. They watched the candle flicker and burn. It made Raymond sleepy so he went upstairs with his Dad, brushed his teeth and then got tucked into bed.

"I love stormy days, Dad," he said sleepily. "I can hardly wait for Christmas to get here!" Raymond fell asleep and dreamed of warm cookies, milk and of course, pink eggs too!

The End

Grandma Hein's Gingersnaps

¾ cup Crisco shortening (not liquid), or butter

1 cup sugar

2 cups flour

2 tsp. baking soda

1 tsp. cloves

¼ cup molasses

1 beaten egg

¼ tsp. salt

1 tsp. cinnamon

1 tsp. ginger

Cream shortening and sugar. If you use butter, it will make thinner, crispier cookies. Add molasses and egg. Beat well. Add dry ingredients. Roll in small 1 inch sized balls, dip in sugar and place 2 inches apart on greased cookie sheet. Bake at 375 degrees for 10 minutes. Cool. Freezes well (but can still be eaten frozen by cookie monsters). Makes 48 cookies.

2. "Away in a Manger"

I hate Mondays, thought six-year-old Trystan as he walked home from school. Even though the sun was shining and it was a beautiful winter day, he did not notice. He walked with his head hung low and dragged his backpack behind him.

Each step seemed to weigh on him more as he thought about what had just occurred before they had been dismissed from school for the day. *How could this have happened? Mrs. Bell must really hate me,* he thought.

Suddenly, he heard his name being called. He turned around and saw Taylor running after him with a huge smile on her face. Taylor lived across the street from him and was in Mrs. Bell's class too.

In a panic, he started to run . . . as he took off he heard her cry, "Trystan, wait!"

He ignored her and ran even faster all the way home. It was a little slippery but he did not even notice as he was so determined to avoid that Taylor girl. She was always smiling at him in the goofy way girls did and she was always asking him to play silly games with her, like dolls or house. He didn't want to play with her and her silly dolls.

Trystan got to the back door of his house and burst inside slamming the door behind him.

He was peeling off his coat when he heard his Mom call out from the kitchen, "Hi, honey! Welcome home."

He ran into the kitchen and went straight up to his Mom, hugging her legs and then he started to cry.

"What's wrong, Trystan? Why are you so upset?" she asked.

"Mom, it's just awful! Mrs. Bell told me I have to play Joseph in the school Christmas play and I don't want to be stupid Joseph. I have to say lines and dress all funny too. I wanted to be the Drummer Boy."

His Mom knelt down in front of him, grabbing him close. "Oh, honey," she said. "It is a huge honour for Mrs. Bell to ask you to portray Joseph. He was a great man with a wonderful, loving heart that trusted in God."

"He was?" Trystan whimpered.

"Yes, indeed, Son. Joseph loved his wife very much. He stood up to a lot people and faced great ridicule from so many people, including his own family. Despite this, he stayed true to his belief in God and in his love for Mary."

"What does ridicule mean, Mom?"

"Well, Trystan, I guess you could say he was bullied by the other men in his town."

Trystan wiped away his tears and caught his breath. With a little hiccup and a tremble of his lip he said, "There's more, Mom. It's even worse . . . Taylor is going to be Mary. I don't want a wife and if I did, it would not be her!"

His Mom laughed out loud at that. "Why don't you go wash your hands and come back, sit down and I can tell you all about Mary and Joseph while I finish making these rolled Oat Cookies. I will cut up an apple for you and even heat up some of your caramel dipping sauce, okay?"

"Okay. I guess," Trystan said.

As he sat on the kitchen stool eating and dunking his apple pieces, his Mom told him all about this Joseph guy and his wife Mary and the birth of their son Jesus. Trystan knew about Jesus from Sunday school. He kind of remembered hearing that he was born in a barn too, but really had not paid much attention to the finer details. Even though he sounded like an okay guy from what his Mom told him, he was still disappointed.

When Mrs. Bell told them about the play they would be in for Christmas and described all the parts available, he had wanted to be the Little Drummer Boy. The Drummer Boy got to beat on a really cool drum that Mrs. Bell had shown them. She also showed them angel wings, which the girls in his class got all silly about and something called a "staff" that the shepherds got to carry.

Even that would have been cool, he thought. Joseph had no props . . . he just got to walk around with his wife Mary, beside a donkey. The donkey was not even real, it was just a large stuffed animal.

"Mom, thanks for telling me all that, but what about ALL these lines I have to learn? I will never get them right."

"Yes, you will, Trystan. I, along with Mrs. Bell, have every confidence in you. Not only can you learn these lines, you can be the best Joseph ever. Show me the lines and we can start practicing right now," she said.

Still not convinced, he slowly hopped off the stool and went to get his backpack. He pulled out the booklet Mrs. Bell had given to each of them that had to speak in the play. On the cover was a picture of Mary, Joseph, and the baby Jesus. Joseph was looking at Mary and she was looking at the baby. They both had kind of a mushy look on their faces, like the looks he saw Dad and Mom give each other sometimes. Above the three of them was a huge star that shone down on them with little lines shooting out from it.

Trystan and his Mom read through the entire play. At one point he read the part where he was supposed to hold Mary's hand. *Yuck!*

"Mom, I don't want to hold Taylor's hand. She gets goofy around me all the time."

Again, his Mom laughed at him. "Trystan, I think Taylor just likes you and wants to be your friend. Girls sometimes show things differently than boys do. You just smile back, that's all. Now, you remember what your hockey coach says? That practice makes perfect. Just like practicing you're skating and shooting, you are going to practice these lines with me each night from now until the day of the play, okay my little Romeo? Like all things we do in life, God just wants us to dedicate ourselves to the task at hand and to do our very best. It's like these cookies, Trystan. They are really not the easiest cookies to bake but each year I make them the best that I can because they are your Grandpa's favourite."

So, practice they did. Each night Mom played Mary and Trystan practiced being Joseph. One night Mom even put a towel around his head held in place with a bungee cord and she put a scarf over her head. That was funny and made Dad laugh too.

Three weeks later the big day arrived and Trystan had to admit he was excited. He had practiced at home with his Mom and at school with Mrs. Bell and the entire class. Yesterday, they even had what Mrs. Bell called a dress rehearsal. When he heard her say that the first time, he thought he was going to have to wear a dress! When he finally did get to try on his costume, it was kind of cool. He even got to wear a fake beard and just like at home, he had a piece of cloth over his head with a cord tied around it. Taylor's costume was a blue robe. Even Trystan thought it looked good on her because it matched her big blue eyes.

When he first stepped out on stage and saw all those people in the audience he kind of froze for a moment, but then Taylor grabbed his hand and gave it a squeeze. He looked at her and smiled, and then they took their positions by the donkey. The play was over quite quickly and the only thing that went wrong was that one of the Kings forgot his line. Mrs. Bell whispered it to him though from the side of the stage where she was standing and smiling at them.

Trystan loved the big, shiny star that hung from above. It was covered in tinfoil and glowed in the lights, just like the cover of his play book. His favourite part of the play was all the applause at the end. He stood up with Taylor and took a bow, just as Mrs. Bell had taught them. When he saw his Mom and Dad in the front row whistling and clapping, sporting goofy faces, he realized what that look was. It meant, "I love you". He smiled back with a special wink for his Mom.

The End

Grandma Hein's Date Filled Rolled Oat Cookies

Date Filling:
    1 cup dates
    1 cup sugar
    1 cup cold water

Boil for a few minutes. Remove from stove. Add 1 tbsp. of flour. Boil until thick, then cool and add 1 tsp. vanilla

Cookie Dough:
    1½ cups rolled oats
    1 cup flour
    ½ cup Crisco shortening
    ½ cup brown sugar
    ¼ tsp. baking powder
    ½ tsp. baking soda
    1 tsp. salt

Mix cookie dough like pastry. Add ¼ cup water. Roll, cut and bake at 350 degrees until they firm up and lightly brown. Note: cut half the dough into a basic round shape. You will need a sharp metal cookie cutter as it is challenging to cut through the oats. For the other half, Grandma used a donut cutter so that the top round cookie had a hole in the middle and the date filling showed through. When cooled, fill a top and a bottom round with date spread in between. Only makes a dozen or so filled cookies but freeze well and they are amazing! Tip: don't make them too big as they are very filling.

3. "All I want for Christmas"

Madeline and her new best friend Emma both watched the small hand of the classroom clock slowly jump towards the number twelve on top. Three, two, one . . . suddenly the school bell clanged loudly, telling them it was lunch hour. The two girls leaped from their desk, ran to their lockers and grabbed their lunch bags.

Madeline and Emma had sat next to each other for three weeks now since Emma had arrived in their grade two classroom one day. Their teacher, Mrs. Berry, had introduced Emma to the rest of the class and explained that she and her Mom had just moved to town. She told the children that they should make Emma feel welcome. She then had Emma sit down in the empty seat next to Madeline. At recess that first day, Emma had hung back in the school yard looking quite lonely and lost. Madeline had noticed this and quickly ran up and invited her to play tag with her and some of the other girls. Emma had smiled at Madeline and quickly joined in the fun.

Madeline thought Emma was a very pretty girl, especially when she smiled, although it seemed that did not happen very often. She had long, dark hair and big, brown eyes, which reminded Madeline of one of her dolls. For the last three weeks, the girls always played together at recess, sat next to each other in the library and made sure they ate lunch together too. They even got to see each other on Sundays because Emma and her Mom had started going to their Church.

Madeline liked to sit near the window in the lunchroom so they could see outside while they ate. Today, the snow was gently falling in big fluffy flakes. After they found two seats at their favourite table, the girls opened up their lunch bags and Madeline started to talk about Christmas. Last night Madeline had spent more time poring over the Wish Book catalogue, dreaming of all the toys that were shown on the glossy pages. Her Mom said she was going to wear the pages out soon.

"What are you asking Santa for this year, Emma?" Madeline asked.

Emma only shrugged her shoulders in reply as she pulled out her jam sandwich and an apple from her brown paper bag.

"Well, I am asking him for a new set of skates, a new doll, a doll's house and clothes for her, an art set, a telescope and a new bicycle," Madeline announced with glee.

Emma's eyes got round as she listened to her new friend's wish list. "Wow, Maddie that is a lot of gifts to ask for. I wish I had a pair of skates so we could go skating together some time."

She then watched Madeline pull out a ham and cheese sandwich, carrots, a pudding and two cookies with sprinkles on them from her pink lunch bag.

As Madeline unwrapped her sandwich she noticed Emma staring at her pile of food. She then looked over at the sandwich and apple Emma had in front of her. The sandwich was all mushy and the apple looked brown and bruised. Emma had not touched either yet.

"Don't you like your sandwich, Emma?"

"Oh yes, I do indeed. My Mom made me a jam sandwich today because I asked her when she was going to bake my favourite Christmas cookies. They are called Jam Jams and I love them. Mom said she did not know if she could bake them for me this year though since she has no money for extras since we left Dad's house," Emma quietly explained. She picked up her sandwich and began to eat it slowly.

"Oh, that is too bad, Emma. My Mom has been baking cookies now for weeks. Tonight she is going to do Christmas cards and she said I can write my letter to Santa at the same time. She is going to mail them all tomorrow. I sure hope he gets it in time."

All too soon the warning bell rang and the girls were back in the classroom for the afternoon. Madeline could hardly sit still as she was anxious to get home so she could write her letter. After what seemed an eternity, the day was done and Madeline hurried home as fast as she could, wading through the newly fallen snow.

Her Mom was there waiting for her and had a snack laid out while she unpacked her back pack. She did her homework, set the table while her Mom made dinner and then played a game on her computer until Dad arrived home.

After they had eaten and cleaned up the kitchen, Madeline sat down at the kitchen table. Her Mom had turned the TV to a music station and Christmas songs played softly in the background. On the table was a box of Christmas cards that had a picture on the front of a beautiful shining star all in glitter. Maddie thought they were beautiful. Beside them lay Mom's address book and a roll of stamps along with her cup of tea. She gave Madeline a blank sheet of paper and a special red pen to write her letter to Santa.

"Okay, sweetie, make sure you print very clearly so Santa can read it," her Mom said with a smile.

"I will, Mommy. I know exactly what I am going to ask him for!" She proceeded to name off all the things she was going to write in her letter.

Her Mom listened to Madeline, frowning a little.

"Madeline, instead of asking for all of that, which I am sure Santa already knows, why don't you take this opportunity to think of something that someone you know really needs? Christmas is about the joy of giving gifts, not getting them. God gave us the gift of his son Jesus, which is why we celebrate this special day."

Madeline frowned a little, deep in thought and chewed on the end of the pen. Suddenly she smiled.

"Mom, I know what I am going to ask Santa for. My new friend Emma needs a pair of skates. She told me her Mom had no money for extras since they left their Dad's house. She told Emma she could not make her favourite jam cookies for Christmas. Instead, she made her a mushy jam sandwich today, and the only treat she had in her bag was an old apple. Would that be something that someone needs, Mom?"

Tears welled up in her Mom's eyes and she smiled and said, "Yes, dear, that is a very worthy wish to ask Santa for."

Maddie got to work and wrote Santa her letter wishing that Emma's Mom had all the things she needed to make some Christmas cookies and for Emma to receive a pair of shiny new white figure skates. When she was done, her Mom read her letter and then helped her fold it up, put it in the envelope and told Maddie what to write on the front:

Mr. Santa Claus
General Delivery
North Pole
H0 H0 H0

Maddie then took a stamp and placed it very carefully on the front of the envelope, and then put it on top of the stack of cards her Mom had written.

"Mom, how will I know that Santa gets my letter?"

"Well, you will just have to ask Emma what she got from Santa when you see her at Church after Christmas."

Later, after tucking Madeline into bed and reading her a story, Mom made a few phone calls then added a few things to her own shopping list.

As Mom and Dad turned out the lights for the night, Mom noticed that some of the glitter from her Christmas cards had magically found its way onto the front of Madeline's letter to Santa. She smiled at the sight.

A few weeks later, after a glorious Christmas, Madeline and her parents went to Church on the Sunday before New Year's. After the service they waited in line to speak to the Reverend. As they stepped up to wish him a Happy New Year, Emma suddenly ran up to Madeline.

"Madeline, Madeline, you will never guess what happened! A big box of gifts was dropped off on Christmas Eve with a Christmas tree. My Mom got all kinds of baking supplies and cookie sheets too! And then on Christmas morning there was a new pair of skates for me from Santa under the tree! Can you skate with me today?"

"I got new skates too," said Madeline. She looked to her Mom for an answer about whether or not she could go skating.

"Of course you can, my dear. I am sure your Dad will take you both over to the rink."

Her Mom and the Reverend then shared a special smile as they watched the two little girls run over to Emma's Mom, excited to share their plans for the afternoon. Madeline's parents followed them over and then invited Emma and her Mom to dinner that night after skating.

The girls had a wonderful afternoon breaking in their new skates with only a few falls, followed by a cup of hot chocolate and cookies that Emma's Mom had baked and brought as a hostess gift. They played with Madeline's new doll's house until both families sat down for a great dinner. Madeline said grace that night.

"Dear Lord, thank you for my new friend Emma and please give Santa a special thank you too, for reading my letter. Amen."

Magic, indeed!

The End

Grandma Hein's Jam Jams

A very basic, plain cookie, but somehow, this one has topped the list of favourites for four generations of kids in our family.

2 eggs
6 tbsp. Rodgers Golden Corn Syrup
1 cup brown sugar
2 tsp baking soda
1 cup shortening
1 tsp vanilla
Flour (enough until it forms a dough ball)

Mix all ingredients together. Flour counter surface and roll dough to ¼ inch thick. Cut in shapes, making sure you have an equal number of each shape. Bake at 350 degrees for 6 minutes. While warm, put two cookies together with raspberry or strawberry jam in between.

4. "Snow Angels"

Eight-year-old Gregory sat in his classroom and watched as the snow kept falling outside. It had started in the morning as he walked to school and had not stopped. When he and the other children had gone outside at recess they had found the new snow to be quite wet, perfect for the snowball fight that had ensued. What fun that was. He was anxious to get home and build a snowman in the front yard because he knew that snow was not always this perfect for snowman making. He just had this last class to get through.

Finally, the bell rung and he was free. He grabbed his backpack, found his coat on the row of hooks in the waiting room, shoved his feet into his boots and jammed his hands into his pockets since his mittens were still very wet from recess. Good thing it was not cold. The two-block walk did not take long and soon he was rushing through the back door of his house.

"Mom, I'm home," he cried as he dropped his backpack in the landing.

"Hi, Son. Did you have a good day?"

"Yeah, it was okay. Mom, I need some carrots and an old hat, quickly. I want to build a snowman before it gets too dark. The snow is perfect."

"Honey, I am afraid that will have to wait. I need you to start shovelling the driveway and sidewalk so your Dad does not have to do it all when he gets home."

"Aw, Mom, that is not fair! Why do I have to do it?"

"Well, I can't very well leave your baby sister alone in the house, now can I? I already checked and Mrs. Miller next door can't watch her either as she is down with a nasty cold. She sounded awful when I spoke to her. So much so, that I made her some soup to take over later. Now, no more arguing, get bundled up and please hop to it my boy. I've got to finish these cookies while your sister is still down for her nap."

Gregory sighed and dug out a new pair of mittens, wrapped a scarf around his neck and went back outside. *Man, oh man, the snow was heavy.* He had the whole driveway full of snow looming ahead of him. As he started in on the task, his mind drifted to how big a snowman he could make, what hat he would use, whether or not he could find an old broom or stick in the shed and finally, what he could use for buttons and the face.

Gregory had shoveled half the driveway when his Dad pulled up.

"Hey there, Greg! Thank you so much for getting started on this, Son. I really appreciate you doing that."

"Sure, Dad. Mom did not leave me much choice about it though. I had wanted to build a snowman but she said I had to do this first. By the time we get done it will be too dark and the snow is perfect today."

"Well, let's see how quickly we can get done, okay? Just let me go in and quickly change and I will be right out to help."

Soon, Gregory's Dad emerged from the house in his ski jacket and boots. He grabbed a shovel and started on the other half of the driveway.

"Greg, I hate to tell you this but I don't think we will have time for your snowman today. Mom says we need to be Snow Angels and shovel off Mrs. Miller's driveway too. Mom said she is really sick and without Mr. Miller this year, she has no one else to help her out."

Gregory groaned and kissed the dream of making a snowman goodbye. He told himself that it probably would have just melted tomorrow anyway. Meanwhile his Dad started whistling while he pushed and heaved the heavy snow. Gregory joined in.

Before Gregory knew it, they were done cleaning their driveway, the sidewalk, and Mrs. Miller's driveway and steps too. He liked working with his Dad and they usually had some funny conversations, but tonight the whistling was about all they could muster.

When they trudged back to door of their house, his Dad grabbed his keys to move his car off the street. Gregory's Mom was waiting at the back door with a plastic container of soup and some star-shaped sugar cookies all wrapped up.

"Greg, please take these over to Mrs. Miller. Ring the doorbell and make sure you hand this to her. Don't just leave it on the step, okay?"

"Aw, Mom, I don't want to go over there. Her house smells like old people."

"Gregory! What a thing to say. Christmas is going to be really hard for Mrs. Miller this year because it will be the first without Mr. Miller. She also told me her kids are not able to come back home so soon after travelling here for the funeral. Think about what that must be like to spend Christmas all alone. Christmas is all about giving, Gregory. This is the least we can do for Mrs. Miller. Now, get going!"

Feeling quite chastened, Gregory took the soup and sugar cookies next door. It was already getting quite dark outside. He rang the bell and soon Mrs. Miller answered the door. Gregory had to admit that she did look sick.

"Hi, Mrs. Miller. Mom told me to give you this soup and these cookies. I hope you feel better soon," he added.

"Why, Gregory, how kind of your Mom. I saw you and your Dad shovelling all that snow off my driveway too. You must know what a relief that is for me, young man. Mr. Miller used to do the shovelling and get the outside of the house ready for Christmas. Since I won't be doing any outside decorating, I'm wondering, would you like to have the big snowman we usually put in the front yard?"

Gregory's eyes grew round with excitement. He knew that snowman well as he had looked at it each and every Christmas with awe since he could remember. It was at least six feet tall and made of crusty white plastic. It glowed when it was plugged in.

"Oh, Mrs. Miller, I really would like to have that snowman. That would be awesome! I was going to make one today for the front yard."

"Wonderful. Why don't you and your Dad go grab it out of the shed, then? It will be nice for me to see it lit up in your front yard."

Gregory ran home, told his parents the exciting news and grabbed his Dad to help him retrieve the snowman from Mrs. Miller's shed. It only took them five minutes to grab it from next door, set it in place and plug it in with an extension cord. Standing back to admire it with his Dad's arms around his shoulders, he looked up to smile at him and noticed a bright shining star twinkling in the sky.

"Well, Son. I think you can see that it pays to put others' needs first, doesn't it? Being a good neighbour by lending a helping hand is the easiest, most rewarding gift you can give."

Dad tousled his head and together they went inside to get warm. Hot soup, salad and fresh bread. Of course, they also had a few sugar cookies too before bed.

The End

The Best Sugar Cookie Recipe (in my humble opinion)

2/3 cup butter, softened
¾ cup granulated sugar
1 tsp baking powder
¼ tsp salt
1 egg
1 tbsp. milk
1 tsp vanilla
2 cups all-purpose flour

In a large mixing bowl, beat butter with an electric mixer on medium to high speed for 30 seconds. Add sugar, baking powder and salt. Beat until combined. Beat in egg, milk and vanilla until combined. Beat in as much of the flour as you can with the mixer. Using a wooden spoon, stir in any remaining flour. Divide dough in half. Cover and chill for about 2 hours or until dough is easy to handle.

Preheat oven to 375 degrees. On a lightly floured surface, roll 1 dough portion at a time to 1/8 to ¼ inch think. Cut cookies into desired shapes. Place 1 inch apart on ungreased cookie sheet. Bake for 7–10 minutes or until edges are very light browned. Cool and decorate. Makes 36 cookies.

5. "Comfort & Joy"

Christopher knew he was supposed to hurry home from school that day, but found some of the other boys in his Grade 5 class in a wickedly intense snowball fight in the school yard. It had snowed heavily the day before and he and his friends were dying to have a huge snowball fight. He hesitated for only a moment before jumping in the game, ducking behind one side of the snow wall that the boys had built.

His best friend Nolan grinned at seeing him dive into the game. "Hey, I thought you were supposed to be going to dish out food with your Mom?" he said.

"Yeah, but I can't miss out on this chance to get those guys," Chris replied as he dodged a ball that flew over his shoulder. He lobbed one back across the yard and managed to get Kevin right in the head.

Snowballs flew back and forth amidst the laughter and screams. Time flew by. Chris was just about to lob another when he heard a car in the school parking lot honking its horn. He paused, looked over and saw his Mom's van.

"Oh no, I've got to go, guys. Do not let them win this war!"

Chris stood up, retrieved his back pack and hurried over to the van. He dodged a few snowballs on the way and arrived at the passenger door with a big grin on his face. It soon disappeared as he saw his Mom's face.

"Chris, get in and buckle up. I specifically told you to hurry home today. Why on earth did you ignore my instructions?"

"Sorry, Mom. I just had to stop and join in the war. The guys needed me."

"Well, there is a homeless shelter that needs us right now, too. We have to be there in just ten minutes, buddy. I had a bowl of Chili all ready for you for supper. You are now going to have to wait to eat until we get home".

"What? I can't go a whole three more hours before I eat supper," he moaned.

"Well, maybe that will help you understand what all these people we are going to feed tonight feel, day in and day out."

He sighed and decided to stay quiet for the rest of the ride. It did not take Mom long to get downtown to the shelter and find a parking spot. They hurried in through the kitchen door.

Chris was not sure what he was expected to do here, but he was impressed at the size of the kitchen. There was a lady who was obviously in charge who came up to them with a smile.

"Well, hello! You must be Jacquie and Christopher. My name is Nancy. Welcome to the Fifth Street Shelter."

Chris's Mom shook her hand, apologized for being late and then they both followed her into the kitchen. There were about five other people working away at various stations. Nancy introduced them to the others and then showed them where they could wash up. When they finished, she handed them aprons to put on and some kind of cap she called a hair net.

"We are running a bit behind. Chris, I thought you could butter the bread for us tonight. Just butter one side and then put each loaf back in its bag. That way it will stay fresh until we serve it." She took him over to a counter that had twenty loaves of bread stacked up to one side and a big bowl of butter on the other side with a big flat knife.

Chris's eyes went wide at the mountain of bread before him. He swallowed down a bit of fear at the task before him and looked questioningly up at his Mom.

She smiled encouragingly at him and said, "You can do this, honey."

Mom was tasked with making huge bowls of salad, so Nancy led her across the kitchen to the salad station.

As Chris dug in and started buttering bread he got into a routine and, just like the snowball fight earlier, time flew by.

The kitchen had a big, long window on one side with big trays of water that were starting to steam. As he finished up his task he watched Nancy slide big metal trays of food over the steaming water. She then lifted off the tin foil that was covering each. There was a tray of meatloaf, all sliced up, a tray of mashed potatoes and a tray of mixed vegetables. The kind that had those yucky lima beans in them that Chris hated to eat. Next was a big vat of gravy, then one of the salad bowls his Mom had made. Nancy then stacked up his twenty loaves of buttered bread and opened one bag. At the very end were huge tins of canned fruit cocktail. Chris's stomach started to rumble in hunger as he smelled the hot food.

On the other side of the counter was a huge dining hall with tables and chairs. On the far side of the room was an old piano and a scraggly looking Christmas tree that had no decorations on it.

"Okay everyone, here is the routine. The doors of the shelter will open in five minutes. Please put on a pair of these gloves." She then told each of them what they would be doing. His Mom was told to ladle a half scoop of gravy over the meat and potatoes on each tray as people went by and he was told to place a piece of bread on top. Nancy herself would man the dessert station on his other side.

"Before the doors open each night, I ask the volunteers to gather and join me in prayer."

They gathered around, bowed their heads while Nancy led them in a prayer thanking God for the food they were about to serve and asking him to keep all those who were still on the street safe that night.

The clock struck six o'clock and a man opened two big doors to the dining hall. People poured in through the doors and formed a line. They grabbed a tray which had little compartments built in it. Each volunteer filled the compartments as the people shuffled along the assembly line.

The first man to go through the line looked scary, Chris thought. He had a scruffy beard and an old scarf wrapped tight around his neck. As Chris laid a piece of bread on his tray the man looked at Chris and smiled at him.

They stood there for over an hour handing out food. Chris wondered if the line would ever stop. They just kept coming. There were old men, young men, women and children too. People in all sizes and shapes. He could not believe that all these people lived on the streets and had no home. Some looked at him, some did not. Some thanked him, some did not say a word.

At one point a mother and her son went through the line. The son was about Christopher's age. When Christopher went to hand him his piece of buttered bread, the boy looked at him and then gave him a huge grin and said, "Thank you!"

Christopher watched the boy and his mother walk away to find a table and thought to himself, *Wow, that could be me and my Mom.*

As the big trays of food were emptied, a worker was right there to take it away and load in another. Chris wondered at one point if they were going to run out? When the last tray of meatloaf was about half done, the line finally ended.

"Great job everyone!" said Nancy. "By my estimation we had about 200 dinner guests tonight."

"Oh my, is that usual, Nancy?" said Chris's Mom.

"No, that is about a third less than usual. The weather has been quite warm, so we don't tend to see as many guests when that happens. Now, our next task is to go out and collect the trays. We use these carts to do that. Jacquie, Chris, why don't you man one cart together?"

It took them about a half-hour to gather up the trays and cutlery, take them into the kitchen and stack them into a huge dishwasher that Chris thought was really cool. It washed them so quickly!

When the kitchen was all clean and tidy, Nancy suggested they all head out to the dining hall. A man was playing some Christmas music on the piano. She and the other staff hauled out two large plastic bins from a storage room. They opened the lids and inside were boxes of old ornaments. They were nothing like what they used at home. The staff then invited all the children in the room to gather around and hang ornaments on the tree, which they did quite happily.

Chris and his Mom watched the kids add the decorations to the tree. When they ornaments were all gone, Nancy called him over and asked him if he would put the special star on the top of the tree.

"You were such a help to us tonight, Chris. We don't usually have children volunteer to help. It was so nice of you to come share this time with us," she said.

"Thank you, Nancy, but I think there is another boy who would really like to put the star on top."

Chris pointed out the boy and his mother that he had seen go through the line earlier. Nancy smiled at him for making the suggestion and then walked over to the boy. Chris watched as Nancy asked him and a huge smile lit up his face. He watched as the boy walked over, climbed the stool someone had placed next to the tree and reached up to place the star on top. When he was done, they took the stool away and then another volunteer plugged the tree in.

The tiny multi-coloured lights shone brightly and everyone stopped talking in the room and turned to admire the tree. The man playing the piano started to play and sing "Oh Come All Ye Faithful". Everyone joined in and sang along. The star on top of the tree seemed to glow magically from the lights below.

After that, Chris and his Mom said their goodbyes, gathered their coats and headed to their car.

"Well, son, I am very proud of you for coming with me and helping these people out tonight. And I am especially proud of you for giving that boy the chance to finish off the tree."

Chris smiled and said, "Mom, I'm very sorry I did not come home right away today. I was being selfish. Thank you for setting this up. Can we do it again next year?"

She smiled at him as she started the car. "Honey, there is no need to wait until next Christmas to volunteer. Tonight I signed us up to help again in January. I am glad you found it rewarding, Christopher. Giving to others is what Christmas is all about and I am so happy we got to share this time together. Now, let's get you home for some Chili, a bath and bed."

The End

Mom's Chili

This is a perfect Chili at any time of the year, but the cloves in it do make for a
great dinner when you are dashing madly about during the holiday season.

1 lb. ground beef
1 onion chopped
3 tbsp. oil
1 green pepper, chopped
1 can of red kidney beans with liquid
1 large can tomatoes
3 or 4 whole cloves
1 or 2 tbsp. of chili powder
1 ½ tsp. salt
1/8 tsp. paprika
1/8 tsp. cayenne pepper
1 bay leaf

Brown onion, green pepper and beef in hot oil. Drain. Add tomatoes, beans and seasoning. Simmer 2 hours adding water if necessary. I sometimes throw in a can of drained, sliced mushrooms and/ or niblet corn. Great served with corn meal muffins.

6. "A Home for the Holidays"

Jess stood in the doorway of her parent's bedroom and watched as her Mom got ready for the Christmas party that was being held that evening. Jess's parents would be going to the party with her Aunt and Uncle. Her Mom stood in front of her full-length mirror holding up first one dress and then another. She frowned at her reflection with each dress held up to her.

"Jess, what do you think? The green one or the black one?" Her Mom turned and held up each dress in front of her so that Jess could see them both.

"The green one, Mom. It's festive and bright and it is a Christmas party after all. You wear the black one every time you go out."

"You are right, my dear; the green one it is. Are you all set to go, honey? Your Dad will be home soon and after he changes we have to hurry over to your Aunt Jamie's house to drop you off."

"Yes, I am all ready to go, although I am not sure I am ready to babysit, Mom. Do you really think I am old enough? I know I kind of pressured Aunt Jamie to let me look after Grayden and Qwynn tonight, but now I am having second thoughts. What if they won't listen to me or go to bed when I tell them to?"

Her Mom looked up from the bed where she sat pulling on her hose.

"Jess, trust me, you are more than ready to babysit and neither I nor your Aunt Jamie would have agreed to this if we did not have every confidence in you, honey. The girls will be just fine. They love their big cousin Jess and would do anything you asked them to. Besides, I happen to know that Aunt Jamie has got a great activity planned for all three of you tonight."

With that said, her Mom hurried into her bathroom to finish her hair and make-up.

"Jess, would you be a dear and please go run the lint brush over my coat? I can't go out tonight with cat hair all over me."

Jess turned and headed downstairs, stopping to grab her backpack from her room on the way. Inside she had packed her booklet from the babysitting class she had taken that summer at the YMCA, along with a couple of her favourite Christmas movies to watch after she got her cousins to bed. Jess had turned twelve a few months ago and was eager to start earning more money. Her Mom had suggested she take the course this summer so that she could start to babysit on the weekends.

She pulled her Mom's coat out of the closet, ran the lint brush over it and placed it on the stairwell banister.

Her Dad walked into the house from the garage and said, "Hey, Jess-Jess, there's my girl. How was your day? Ready for the weekend?"

He walked over to her and gave her a hug and headed up the stairs as she replied, "It was okay, Dad, and yes, I guess I am ready."

When her parents finally came downstairs, they both looked so elegant. Her Mom in her green party dress that matched the colour of her eyes and her Dad in his black suit.

She whistled at them both, "Looking good, guys!"

They all got into their car and drove the short distance to her Aunt and Uncle's house. When they walked through the front door her two little cousins launched themselves at her with shrieks of delight. Being only six and four, her two cousins were full of energy.

With the two girls holding her hands, she followed Aunt Jamie into the kitchen.

"Now, Jess, I have just a couple of things to show you. Here is a list with my cell number and Uncle Tyler's cell number, along with the number for the house we will be at tonight. The girls have had their supper already so all they need is a yoghurt maybe before bed, which is in two hours. They like to have their snack in the living room so they can watch the Christmas tree before bed. After that, you know the drill: bathroom, teeth and a story. I baked the gingerbread house pieces today so that you can all build the house together tonight."

Jess smiled with anticipation and thanked her Aunt for taking the time to set this all up for her. On the island were pieces of gingerbread: two sides, two ends and two roof pieces along with a big bowl of white icing and tons of candy decorations all laid out in their own little bowls. There were jelly beans, red and green gummies, pretzels in long and round shapes along with little silver balls and so much more. It looked like a candy store!

"Wow, Aunt Jamie, this looks amazing. Thank you so much. This will be lots of fun, right girls? Your Mom used to always do this with me each Christmas when I was your age."

Grayden and Qwynn nodded yes in unison and started jumping up and down, "When can we start?"

"As soon as you say goodnight to your parents."

Jess watched as the girls both got big hugs and kisses from their Mom and Dad at the front door.

Her own Mom walked over and gave her shoulder a big squeeze and said, "I am proud of you Jess; you will be AWESOME! Just remember to have fun."

The parents left and Jess locked the front door behind them.

"Okay, peanut one and two, let's go build a house."

She got the girls to wash their hands, don their aprons and they helped her squirt a line of icing on both sides of the inside back edge of the house. Qwynn gently held one side tight against the back wall, while Grayden and Jess held the other side. After about five minutes, the three pieces all stayed standing. They repeated the process with the front of the house. Once that set, they tackled adding the roof slabs. Those were a bit more of a challenge, but they persevered. At one point she had to leave Grayden pressing the sides together while she helped Qwynn go to the bathroom and wash her hands again.

Soon, they had a bare house standing, ready to be decorated.

She pulled all the candy over and immediately Qwynn declared, "The jelly beans are mine!" as she grabbed the bowl and put her arms around it. Jess watched as Qwynn immediately started popping them into her mouth.

Grayden gave out a cry of frustration and yelled, "Qwynn, you can't eat them now. We have to put them on the house first!"

Qwynn's lip trembled and she started to cry and stomp her feet. Grayden took that opportunity to grab the bowl of jelly beans away from her, which just caused Qwynn to start wailing.

Jess did not know what to do and had a pure moment of panic. Gathering her wits about her she removed the jelly beans and put them on the other side of the kitchen.

"Hey, until you two stop fighting and can agree to share those jelly beans, nothing more is going to be done on this house," she declared.

"That's not fair. I didn't do anything!" Grayden argued.

Jess held Qwynn in a hug, trying to comfort her. Finally, she stopped crying and settled down.

"Now, Qwynn, do you agree to share the jelly beans with Grayden?"

Qwynn tucked her head into Jess's shoulder and just nodded.

"Grayden, do you promise not to yell at Qwynn again? This is the first time she has built a gingerbread house. She doesn't know any better."

"Yeah, okay, Jess, I promise not to yell anymore. Can we please decorate the house now?"

Jess agreed. "I am going to get you each a big bowl and we are going to count out the pieces of candy and you are each going to get the exact same amount, okay? Grayden, you are going to decorate this half of the house and, Qwynn, you and I will work on this other half, agreed?"

Soon, the girls calmed down and Jess started to ask them questions about Christmas to keep them focused. As they dipped their candies in the icing and pressed them onto the house, they told her all about what they hoped Santa would bring them on Christmas morning. They spoke of their favourite decorations on the tree and what they were going to make their parents for gifts.

Before long, the house was done.

"It's beautiful," Grayden said in awe.

"I'm going to live in a house that looks just like that someday," Qwynn proclaimed. The thought of which set all three of them to giggle, imagining Qwynn small enough to fit through the front door that was outlined in pretzel sticks.

As it was just about time for bed, Jess had them help her tidy up, wash their hands and then she went to pull two yoghurts from the fridge.

Oh no, Jess thought to herself. There was just one cherry and one peach container left. Well, maybe one of them did not like one of those flavours.

"Who wants cherry and who wants peach?" she asked.

Qwynn smiled. "Jess," she said. "Can you give us half of each flavour so we can share them?"

"Yes, of course, Qwynn. Great idea!"

The girls took their bowls of yoghurt into the living room and kneeled in front of the coffee table. While they ate their yoghurt they all looked at the Christmas tree. It was decorated all in red and green with shiny white lights. On the very top of the tree was a star made of glitter. It seemed to glow from the lights below.

Soon, it was bedtime for her little cousins. Jess took them upstairs and supervised them in the bathroom, then got them changed into their jammies and tucked them into their twin beds.

"Story, story," they both chanted.

Jess smiled as she stood in front of their book shelf. She pulled a book out and said, "I have the perfect fairy tale for you tonight, girls . . ."

Soon, they were enthralled as they listened to Jess tell them about another candy house and a young brother and sister named Hansel and Gretel who shared a thin twig to trick the bad witch.

After they were asleep Jess turned out the lights and went downstairs feeling quite proud of herself. She curled up on the couch and watched one of her movies while she waited for the parents to get home.

Not long after her movie ended she heard a key in the front door and her Aunt, Uncle, Mom and Dad strolled in. They went into the kitchen to make coffee, and Jess told them about her eventful evening; the girls fighting over the candy, and how she had panicked for a moment, not knowing what to do.

"Oh, Jess, I am so sorry Grayden and Qwynn misbehaved," her Aunt Jamie said. "We are trying to teach Qwynn about sharing and what you did was the perfect solution."

Once the adults were finished drinking their coffee and had made plans to spend Sunday dinner together, Jess and her parents got ready to go home. As Jess was putting on her coat her Uncle Tyler handed her a crisp new $20.00 bill with a hearty hug of thanks for babysitting their girls.

Jess's eyes lit up when she looked at the bill in her hands. She knew exactly what half of this was going to go towards. She wanted to put her own money into the collection bowl on Sunday so that she too could share what she had with others less fortunate, which is what her Mom and Dad had always told her Christmas was all about.

The End

Carla's Gingerbread

1 cup shortening
¾ cup brown sugar, packed
1/3 cup dark molasses
1 egg
1 tsp. vanilla
2 ¾ cup all-purpose flour
1 tsp. salt
1 tsp. baking powder
1½ tsp. ground ginger
½ baking soda

Cream together shortening, brown sugar, molasses, egg and vanilla. Stir together flour, salt, baking powder, ginger, baking soda. Stir dry ingredients into creamed ingredients.

Shape soft dough into 2 rounds and wrap in waxed paper or clear plastic wrap. Chill thoroughly (at least 30 minutes). Roll out on floured surface and cut with gingerbread man cutter. Or, you can press dough into house forms or cut from a gingerbread house pattern. Bake on ungreased cookie sheet at 350 degrees for 8–10 minutes. Makes about 15 gingerbread men, depending on size of your cookie cutter. Cool and decorate with icing.

7. "A bright Red and Green"

Ten-year-old James was lounging in his pajamas on the couch watching cartoons. It was Saturday morning and he had just finished a wonderful breakfast of fruit and his Mom's cinnamon buns. He had about a half-hour before he had to get ready to go to the rink for his hockey game.

He was just getting into a great episode featuring his favourite action hero when his Dad walked into the room.

"Hey, sport, what do you say about helping me this afternoon put up the Christmas lights? It is not too cold out today so we better make hay while the sun shines."

James looked to his Dad questioningly. "What does that mean, Dad?"

His Dad always had these funny little sayings. James could not see how making hay and stringing Christmas lights were connected at all. *Make hay? That sounded crazy!*

His Dad laughed in response and said, "It just means that there is no point in putting off until tomorrow what you can do today, Son."

"Sure, whatever, Dad. I can help with the lights. Do I get to climb the ladder?"

"No, that would not be safe, James. Remember, safety comes first. What you can help me with though is attaching new clips to the strings and testing the bulbs on each strand. Then I really need you to spot me on the ladder. We should get this done in no time."

With the day suddenly planned out for him, James and his Dad soon set off for the rink. He had packed up his hockey bag the night before and there was lots of equipment inside of it. The bag was so heavy his Dad had to carry it for him to the car, and then into the rink.

As he was getting ready in the dressing room with all of his team mates, he realized he had forgotten his mouth guard. His Mom would be angry with him as she really did not want him to play hockey in fear that he would lose some teeth.

Even though he knew he should tell Coach, James shrugged away his Mom's fears and warnings aside, and followed his team mates out on the ice for the game. His Dad was seated in the stands with a hot coffee, probably talking about "making hay" with the other parents.

Today they were facing off against the number one team in their division. Their coach had told them that if they focused on their defense they could actually beat them, so the boys were all pumped up, eager to practice all the moves Coach had taught them.

James was a great skater and he loved the feel of the ice under his skates, the cold, moist air of the rink and the sounds of the pucks as they hit the boards.

The score was 2-0 for the other guys by the end of the second period. Not good. He could tell that he was not skating aggressively enough because not having his mouth guard was actually bothering him. He could not get his Mom's voice out of his head.

Finally the whistle blew and they made their way off the ice. His Dad gave James a thumbs up from the stands as he skated by him.

As the line of boys made their way to the dressing room with shoulders down in what was sure to be defeat, he saw his Mom standing near the dressing room door.

She smiled at him and held out his mouth guard. "You forgot this, James. I found it on your nightstand when I was making your bed. Now, put that thing in your mouth so I can go home and get my cookie baking started."

He smiled in relief at his Mom. *Now, the world was right!* Feeling enthused he went into the dressing room where Coach immediately reminded them of their strength and ability on the ice.

The third period of the game flew by and James skated like his old self. They won the game! The score was 3-2 and James had even scored the winning goal in the third period. Sadly, one of the boys on the other team had taken a hard hit and fallen face first on the ice. He lost his two front teeth because he wasn't wearing a mouth guard.

After the game, his Dad took him for a hamburger. That was their bargain. If he scored, he got a hamburger at his favourite take-out restaurant. After they ate their burgers and fries they stopped in at the hardware store and picked up replacement bulbs and new clips for the lights.

When they got home, James unloaded his hockey bag and thanked his Mom again for bringing the mouth guard to the rink.

"You know, Mom, you are right. Skating without a mouth guard is just asking for trouble." As he watched her rolling out ropes of dough on the counter he told her all about the boy who lost his teeth.

"Oh no," she gasped. "That poor boy! That could have been you, James. Promise me that if you ever are in that situation again you will not play."

James made the promise and then headed out to the garage where his Dad was already bringing down the box of Christmas lights from the rafters.

They used the work bench and one by one, plugged in each strand. If they found a bulb burnt out, they tried tightening it and if that did not work, they replaced it with either a red or green bulb. Then James helped his Dad fasten on the new clips every foot along the cords. Soon they had all six strands of lights ready to go.

He helped his Dad carry out the ladder to the front yard. His Dad made sure the ladder was propped up and securely planted in the flower bed before he started to climb it to the eaves. He had showed James how to stand at the bottom of the ladder and plant his feet on either side to help stop the ladder from shifting.

One by one, he handed up the strings of lights to his Dad who clipped them into place. The late afternoon sun was shining down on them and they talked about what it was like for his Dad growing up on a farm. The finishing piece to their decorations was a silver star that got nailed into place on the roof above the front door. His Dad had to fuss with that a bit, but all in all, it only took them a couple of hours and then they were done.

James was allowed to flip the switch and they stood back to look at the lights from the street. They were perfectly lined up: red/green/red/green. However, James noticed that the two very centre bulbs hanging under the star were both white.

"How did those white lights get in there, Dad?"

His Dad laughed: "I thought I would put them in there to remind you how important it is to make sure safety comes first. Those two white bulbs are in honour of that boy who lost his two front teeth today."

James giggled, but got the message, loud and clear. The star seemed to shine brighter with the two white bulbs.

They tidied up the work bench and then went inside where Mom had cocoa and some fresh baked Candy Cane cookies waiting for them. It had been a great day of lessons learned.

The End

Carla's Candy Cane Cookies

¾ cup margarine, softened
¾ cup sugar
1 egg
½ tsp. vanilla
2 cups flour
½ tsp. salt
½ tsp. baking powder
½ tsp. peppermint extract
1/3 cup flaked coconut
2 tsp. red food coloring

Cream together margarine, sugar and baking powder, egg and vanilla. Add in flour and salt. Divide dough in half. In one half stir in the coconut. In the other half, add in the peppermint extract and the red food colouring. Cover and chill for 30 minutes.

Divide each portion into 30 little balls. Roll each ball into ropes and twist together with an alternate colour rope. Form into a candy cane shape. Bake at 375 degrees for 10 minutes. Great cookie for little helping hands to work with. Freezes well.

My sister always hung cookies on her tree for her kids and these worked well for that, too!

8. "Simple Pleasures"

McKenzie felt the warmth of the sun on her face as its rays shone through the bedroom window.

As she lay there, gathering her thoughts, a sense of dread came over her. Her Mom and Dad had dropped her off at her Gran's in the country for the weekend so that they could "get some things done".

Being eleven years old she knew what that meant; they would be spending the weekend at the mall shopping, stopping to have some fancy coffees and then maybe going out for a nice dinner. She sighed with envy as she thought of her parents and no doubt, all of her girlfriends, getting into the Christmas spirit at the mall.

"How did I get stuck out here?" she muttered to herself.

It was not that she did not love her Gran to bits, but it was SO boring out here in the country. Her Gran had no wireless connection and did not even own a desktop. To top it all off there was no cell coverage this far out! This was a huge issue because she could not get or receive any texts from her friends. McKenzie lived for her cell phone. She had gotten it for her birthday and was never without it. She felt so isolated here.

Things were bad enough, however, to make matters worse, the power had gone off the night before when they had just settled down to watch "White Christmas", one of Gran's favourite movies. When her Gran had read in the TV Listings section of the newspaper that it was playing that night, she had been so excited. McKenzie guessed it was because Gran only had three TV channels so you must get pretty excited when there was something you wanted to watch. The movie was actually not that bad from what she had been able to see of it.

After the power had gone out, Gran had calmly lit a few candles so that they could see and, after chatting for a while, they both decided to go to bed early in the hope that the power would be back on the following morning.

Having no power meant that McKenzie had been unable to charge her phone to play games. She raised one arm from under the blankets and reached over to the bedside lamp and tried it. Click. Nothing.

"Oh, great. Another day roughing it."

As she lay there feeling sorry for herself, she could hear her Gran rattling around in the kitchen. She was whistling for heaven's sake! *How could she be happy enough to whistle when there was no power?*

Throwing back the covers she was immediately hit by the coldness of the house. YIKES!

I am going to freeze to death out here in the boonies and they won't find Gran and me until spring, she thought.

McKenzie threw on her jeans and sweatshirt, stopped in the bathroom across the hall that was still cast in darkness and then headed downstairs to the kitchen. It was a lot warmer there because Gran had a lit a fire in her fireplace that opened up not only to the kitchen, but also to the living room on the other side.

"Well, there's my sleeping beauty!" Gran exclaimed when she saw her.

"Morning, Gran."

"Now, McKenzie, I am afraid I could not bake your cinnamon buns like I promised you because the oven doesn't work when the power is out, but we always have the gas stove top, so you can have pancakes or eggs, or both. What's it going to be?" Gran asked with a big smile.

"Um, eggs I guess, please."

"Okay, princess, why don't you go up and get changed for Church while I get breakfast made?"

"We're still going to Church, Gran? Do we have to? I thought that with all the snow that fell yesterday afternoon we would just be staying home."

"Oh, McKenzie, a little snow doesn't stop me. That's what trucks are made for."

McKenzie sighed and turned around to head back upstairs. She stopped, turned back and asked Gran what she should wear to Church.

"Oh, anything but blue jeans will be fine. Sunday is supposed to be the one day in the week when you get out of your everyday gear. No grand-daughter of mine is going to Church on the Second Advent in denim."

"Gran, they aren't called blue-jeans anymore . . . just jeans." McKenzie turned with resignation and headed back upstairs to change. Thankfully, her Mom had packed a pair of her leggings and a long sweater that was both comfy and warm.

Right after a great breakfast of eggs, bacon and what Gran called "stove-top toast", essentially a grilled cheese without the cheese, they headed to Church.

McKenzie had been to this Church before of course, as they usually spent Christmas Eve at Gran's. It was a pretty little white building with a wonderful view of the valley below. The sanctuary in the Church had a simple, single star hanging from above. It was beautiful.

The Reverend spoke mostly about the Advent. Specifically, he talked about Mary and the trials she went through . . . travelling long distances on a donkey while being nine months pregnant and how adversity makes you stronger. Then a young girl in the congregation was asked to light the second blue Advent candle. The congregation also sang quite a bit and McKenzie enjoyed that immensely. Back at home, she and her friends sang along with her Karaoke machine quite a bit and everyone said she had a pretty good singing voice.

After her Gran chatted with her friends at the end of the service, they headed back to the farmhouse. The sun was shining brightly and it had turned out to be quite a warm day. While there was not much in the way of buildings in the area, McKenzie had to admit that it was really pretty countryside, especially now so because the trees were all covered with hoar frost. It looked like a layer of sparkling diamonds had been cast over everything.

Gran just owned a couple of acres now with the house on it as she had sold off most of the land to the neighbours when Grandpa had died. McKenzie didn't remember much about Grandpa except his booming laugh and that he was meticulous with his things. He always used to say, "Waste not, want not."

"Gran, do you think the power will be back on at the house now?" McKenzie asked. She had brought her game station with her in high hopes of sitting in front of the TV all weekend getting to the next level of her favourite video game.

"Doubt it," was Gran's honest, blunt reply.

"What am I supposed to do all afternoon until Mom and Dad get here?" she whined.

"McKenzie, honestly, I am disappointed in you. There is a whole bookshelf in the living room filled with books. Why don't you curl up and read while there is daylight? Or, if that is not *exciting* enough for you, why don't you grab the sled from the barn and go sledding down at the hill? You could ask one of the Baker girls next door to go with you. They would love to do that."

"Ask some strangers to go play?" McKenzie asked incredulously.

Gran laughed at that. "McKenzie, they are not strangers. You and Kerry used to play together all the time when you spent your summers here."

McKenzie vaguely remembered playing with Kerry. She had reddish hair and lots of freckles back then. She pondered her options for the afternoon in silence: *read a book or sledding*? She knew what books were in the bookshelf; old stories from when her Mom and Aunts were little. Laura Ingalls Wilder, Nancy Drew and a bunch of others she was not familiar with.

When they got back to the house, Gran made her a sandwich and then said, "Well, kiddo, what are you going to do this afternoon?"

"Go sledding, I guess. What is Kerry's number so I can call her?"

"The phone doesn't work when the power is out. Just grab the sled and go knock on their door the old-fashioned way."

"Really? What if she doesn't remember me, or want to go?" McKenzie asked with a bit of fear.

"Well, then you can go by yourself. It's not like you need to have two people to go sledding."

McKenzie could not fathom the concept of going anywhere alone. With lots of doubts, she changed back into her jeans, pulled on her boots, ski-jacket, toque and mittens. When she entered the kitchen Gran was whistling again and laying out ingredients on the counter.

"Have fun, my dear. Come home before it gets dark though. If you want to invite Kerry back here I can make some hot chocolate for you both and I will have the Peanut Butter Slice ready by then."

McKenzie headed out to the barn and looked for a racer or inner tube amidst the piles of stuff stored in there. She could not see anything but an old wooden sled. It looked ancient! *Gran surely couldn't expect me to use that, could she?* Shaking her head, she grabbed the string and pulled it out and set off down the road.

She could not believe it when Kerry answered the door with a big smile on her face. Still full of freckles, McKenzie could just make the hint of a red curl under her toque.

"I saw you coming down the lane with the sled, McKenzie. I sure hope you want me to go sledding with you?"

McKenzie smiled in reply and soon the girls set out to the big hill below the Baker farm.

She apologized for the condition of her sled, but Kerry just shrugged and said, "Oh, those are the best. I wish we still had ours. It used to go like crazy!"

Sure enough, Gran's old sled was the fastest one on the hill that day. There were lots of kids out sledding and McKenzie had so much fun getting to know Kerry again. They spent two whole hours running up the hill and then speeding back down it at breakneck speeds.

"We should probably get going, McKenzie. It will be dark soon."

"How can you tell? You don't have your phone and you're not even wearing a watch."

"Oh, I just know from the way the light is fading."

The girls headed back to Gran's and sure enough, when they got there Gran had a pot of hot chocolate warming on the stove and a roaring fire going in the fireplace. The girls sipped their chocolate in front of the fireplace and ate some of the amazing Peanut Butter Slice Gran made each Christmas. It was McKenzie's favourite. They told Gran about all their runs down the hill, the other kids that were there and about how amazingly fast Gran's old sled went.

Just as Kerry was getting ready to leave, McKenzie's parents arrived to take her home to the city.

The girls said goodbye to one another. When McKenzie asked Kerry for her cell phone number so they could text, Kerry laughed and said, "I don't have a cell phone, McKenzie. We don't get coverage out here but you can email me or just come over anytime you visit your Gran."

Shaking her head in wonder at how Kerry didn't seem to mind not having a cell phone, McKenzie ran inside and headed upstairs to pack her stuff. It was only then she noticed the power was back on. She could not believe she had just spent a whole day without power and had not even really noticed. She grabbed her phone and threw it in her suitcase. *No need for that until I'm back in the city,* she thought.

Hugging her Gran goodbye, she thanked her for putting up with her and for showing her how to "rough it". They giggled with each other and hugged goodbye. McKenzie could not wait to come back for Christmas to spend more time with Gran and Kerry.

The End

Mom's Peanut Butter Slice

Melt ½ cup brown sugar and ½ cup corn syrup until dissolved. Mix two cups of flaked corn cereal and one cup crisp rice cereal with one cup of peanut butter. Pour syrup mixture over cereal mix. Stir well. Press into 8x8 pan and spread with the Caramel Icing.

Icing:
   ¼ cup butter
   2 tbsp. milk
   ½ cup brown sugar
   1 cup icing sugar
   1 tsp. vanilla

Melt butter and brown sugar over low heat until caramel in colour. Add milk and icing sugar and vanilla. Spread over cake and then allow to cool.

A wonderfully decadent square that only needs the stove top. Freezes really well, too!

9. "Believe!"

Eight-year-old Stuart raced home from school. The only time he slowed down was at the single crosswalk on his usual route home. By the time he got to his block, he was out of breath and a stitch was starting in his side. He did not care though because if he could have sprouted wings and flown home that day, he would have.

Today, he was going to volunteer at an animal shelter. His Mom had made arrangements for them to donate a couple of hours of their time and today was the day. While Stuart realized this was being done just to ease the pain of not being able to have a puppy of his own, he was still excited to go and see the animals.

All year, he had begged and pleaded with his parents to let him have a puppy. They kept saying that he was too young and that it was not the right time to add a dog to the family.

Throughout the year he had hoped that they would change their minds. On his birthday in August, he had been sure he was going to get a puppy. He got an aquarium instead, which was great, but it still wasn't a dog. He had never wanted anything more than he wanted a puppy.

In all the story books he read, a boy always had a dog as his faithful companion beside him. He could close his eyes and see himself playing fetch in the yard with a dog, going for long walks with him, riding his bike with a little furry friend following along and falling asleep each night with his dog laid beside his bed. He had never felt this kind of aching hole in his heart before. His Mom said he was "fixated" about dogs, *whatever that meant!*

He opened the door to his house and rushed inside, barely stopping to kick off his shoes.

"Mom, I'm home!" he bellowed out.

"So I hear," she said with a chuckle. "Go wash your hands and eat the apple and cheese slices I put on the table for you. Supper will be late tonight. I'm just going to load up these boxes into the trunk and then we can head off."

Doing as he was told, he washed his hands and then ate his snack before putting his plate in the dishwasher. He grabbed the last box at the landing and headed outside to help his Mom load up all the blankets and towels they had stacked up the night before. His Mom said that the animal shelter was always looking for old sheets, towels or blankets to use with the animals. He also made sure to grab the container of home-made dog biscuits they had baked the day before.

All loaded up, his Mom locked the house and they set off.

"Mom, how many dogs do you think I will get to play with today?"

"Well, I am sure we will see lots of dogs and cats today, but we are not going there to play with them, we are going there to work. Animals need a lot of care and attention, Stuart, especially dogs."

"Oh, Mom, I know, but I am just so excited to meet them all."

The shelter was not that far away, Stuart noted. He could easily make it there on his bike in the summer.

"Mom, can I volunteer there more than just today?"

"Well, sure, but let us see if you enjoy this first, okay?"

"Oh I will, Mom. No doubt about that."

They pulled in and parked and then he helped his Mom carry in their donations. Once inside, a lady who said her name was Carolyn greeted them and shook their hands. Stuart could hear dogs barking from behind a door.

"Thank you so much for all of these goodies. We sure can use them, especially with January coming up. Why don't you hang up your coats and then you can put on these smocks so that your clothes don't get all mucked up?"

She handed a purple flowered shirt to Stuart, which was really ugly, but he put it on anyway. His Mom got one with bumble bees all over it. Carolyn helped Stuart roll up the sleeves because they were too long for him.

"Why is January so busy for you?" Mom asked.

"Well, sadly, so many people buy puppies for Christmas gifts and then realize how much work they are and end up turning them over to us to adopt out. See that bulletin board? Well, right now there are only twelve dogs and a few cats on it, but come January that will jump to about thirty animals."

Stuart looked at the bulletin board and saw that each dog or cat had a photo pinned up with a name written below it. There were also details for each written below; their weight, the breed, their approximate age and their name, if known. Some didn't have a name written down at all.

"Carolyn, how come some of these dogs and cats have no name?" he asked.

"Well, Stuart, they were strays that someone found and dropped off. Their owners, whomever they were, did not take the time to get them tattooed or micro-chipped when they bought them and so we have no way of knowing who they belong to. We try not to name them while they are here because we want the family who adopts them to name them."

Stuart could not imagine having to give up an animal, or not being able to return it to the owner if it was lost and alone.

"Okay, ready to get started?" Carolyn asked.

Stuart nodded eagerly as she led them through the door behind the desk. As they walked through to the back of the building, the barking got louder and louder. He could see a row of kennels on each side of the room and some of the dogs were jumping up and down as they entered.

As Carolyn opened up each pen and put a leash on the dogs, she handed them to either Stuart or his Mom. She instructed them to walk them back through a swinging gate, and then unleash them in the play area. Carolyn told them there was also a door further back that led them to an outside area that was all fenced off too.

Stuart barely got a chance to pet each of the dogs but he could see there were all types of dogs in different shapes and sizes. There were white dogs, black dogs, multi-colored dogs and even a red haired dog. All but one of them were older dogs. There was just one small dog that Stuart thought was a puppy.

Once the dogs were all in the play area, Carolyn made them put on rubber gloves and showed them how to remove the trays from the bottom of the cages. They then had to carry the heavy trays over to a sink and counter area on the far side of the room. There, they removed all the smelly "messes" and hosed down the trays. She then had Stuart's Mom spray a disinfectant over the tray before laying them back in the kennels.

Once that was done, they were able to take off the gloves. She asked Stuart to take each kennel a bowl of food that she was scooping up. Some bowls had to go to specific cages with different food if the dog had an allergy. The same procedure was followed with the water bowls.

The dogs had started to whine when they heard the food being scooped up. As they led the dogs back to their pens Carolyn shared with them the story of how each dog came to be at the shelter. Some of the stories were very sad. She told them that one of the dogs had even been beaten by its owner. Even now, some six weeks after arriving, scars were still visible on this beautiful, yellow Labrador. Carolyn explained how the shelter's vet had stitched him up as best as he could. When Carolyn went to pet that dog, it cowered away from her touch.

"It is going to take this dog a long time to heal emotionally," she explained.

When it came time to put the puppy back in its kennel, Stuart took a moment to crouch down and pet the dog. It was white and had brown spots all over it and it was very cute. The puppy wound itself through Stuart's legs and then tried jumping into his lap. Its tail was wagging wildly as Stuart petted the dog. He noticed how soft its fur was and that it had dark ears so long they almost dragged on the ground.

Carolyn said that this puppy was only ten weeks old and that it was still really missing his Mom. The owners of the dog that had the litter were able to sell all of the pups but this one and because they were leaving on a holiday, they could not wait around until this last female pup sold. She explained that it was an English Springer Spaniel pup and would grow to just under the height of her knees.

Carolyn and his Mom watched Stuart make friends with the puppy for a while, but then Carolyn said they still had lots to do in the cat room.

Stuart gave the little puppy a final pet and then put it back in its kennel. The puppy whimpered and, as they left the dog room, Stuart gave the pup a final wistful wave goodbye.

They spent the next hour basically going through the same routine in the cat room, but they were able to scoop up the messes from the kitty litter in each cage. Stuart really liked the cats too, but not as much as the dogs.

When they were done for the day, Carolyn thanked them for coming out and said she hoped she would see them again. Stuart hoped so, too.

At dinner that night Stuart excitedly told his Dad all about their time at the shelter. He told him all about the puppy that he had met. After supper he and his Dad went online and read all about English Springer Spaniels. They were really cool dogs, specifically good for bird hunting.

"Dad, wouldn't you love to hunt?" Stuart asked excitedly. "A dog is just what you need to help you retrieve the ducks you shoot."

"Stuart, I don't own a gun and would never want to hunt anything." His Dad chuckled. "Nice try, Son."

"Well, I am still going to ask Santa for a puppy for Christmas," he declared.

A few days later he was surprised to see his Mom and Dad waiting for him in the school parking lot. He got in the car and buckled up.

"Where are we going?" he asked.

"Well, Son, Mom and I thought we would head to the mall and grab some supper there tonight. I just have to make one stop on the way at Brent's house." Brent was an old buddy of his Dad's that would occasionally pop over for a visit.

When they pulled up at the house, his Mom and Dad told him to come in with them. They were going to have a coffee inside with Brent and his wife Kathy. Stuart groaned, because he knew how boring this could be for him.

Once they were inside, a beautiful dog met them with its tail wagging. It looked similar to the puppy at the shelter, but it had black spots instead. It was a male dog and its name was "Skipper".

Skipper and Stuart played with a rope toy while the adults talked. Stuart could vaguely hear them and it seemed they were talking about dog breeds but he didn't really pay them much attention, preferring to play with this wonderful, friendly dog.

At one point Skipper went to the front door and whined a little. Brent came over and put a leash on Skipper because he apparently "had to go". He asked Stuart if he would mind taking Skipper for a walk.

"Sure!"

He took the leash and he and Skipper headed out for a walk. *What a great dog this is*, Stuart thought. He didn't pull on the leash like his friend Darryl's dog did. He took him around the block and made sure to pick up the mess with the little grey bag that Brent had given him. One house they passed on their walk was all covered in lights and had a huge display of figures on the lawn. Stuart and Skipper stopped to look at them all. In front of the display was a blue donation box with a shiny silver star painted on it. The sign next to it said, "Make a donation and your Christmas wish will come true". Stuart dug out a Loonie he had in his pocket, looked longingly at Skipper and then dropped it in the box. They returned to the house after a great fifteen-minute walk.

Brent asked him how the walk went and then said, "Skipper loves his walks. He needs three walks a day; one as soon as he gets up, one around noon, and then one in the evening before bed. You are always welcome to come and take him for a walk, Stuart."

Stuart eagerly nodded: "Oh yes, please!" he said.

The three of them left Brent and Kathy's soon afterwards and headed to the mall for a fun night of shopping and dinner.

As Christmas approached, his Mom would ask him occasionally what he wanted for Christmas and he always just gave her one answer, "A dog, Mom. If I believe hard enough that I will get one, Santa will bring it for me."

His Mom would just give him a smile in return and shake her head.

Soon, it was Christmas Eve. They usually all went to service at Church, but his Dad said he was too busy in the garage to go. When Stuart and his Mom got back from Church they curled up to watch a movie on the couch. His Dad was still in the garage, "being an Elf" his Mom said.

When the movie was over, Stuart laid out cookies for Santa and then got tucked into bed. His Mom kissed him goodnight and reminded him not to go downstairs in the morning until Dad said so.

Stuart awoke early the next day and eagerly jumped out of bed. He raced to his parent's room and shouted, "Merry Christmas, Mom and Dad! Can we go downstairs now, please? I want to see what Santa brought me."

Stuart and his parents headed downstairs, and there, under the tree in a crate with a big red bow on it was the puppy from the shelter.

"See, I told you," said Stuart. "If I believed hard enough, I knew Santa would bring me a puppy."

His Dad helped him open the crate and pull out the happy puppy whose tail was wagging with excitement.

"Well, Stuart, Santa asked your Mom and me to prepare you as best we could before today. He wanted you to be sure you understand what responsibility comes with being a dog owner. She will need to be trained, fed, watered, walked and played with *EVERY* day of her life, Stuart, and that will be up to you to make sure it is done. What are you going to call her, Son?"

"Dixie," he said with absolute conviction. He had read that dog name in a book once and had loved it.

When he opened his other gifts under the tree, there was a book about Spaniels, a gift certificate for him and Dixie to go to puppy training school together and all kinds of other wonderful things for his new dog. It was the BEST Christmas ever!

The End

PB and Banana Dog Treats

1 banana, peeled
1 cup oat flour
2/3 cup rolled oats
½ cup dried parsley (for their breath)
3 tbsp. peanut butter.
1 egg, beaten

Preheat oven to 300 degrees. Put banana in large bowl and mash thoroughly. Add the rest and stir well to combine. Set aside for 5 minutes.

Roll mixture into 24 balls, using about 1 tbsp. dough for each. Bake on cookie sheet lined with parchment paper. Place ball on parchment and use the back of spoon to flatten into a coin shape. Bake until firm and deep golden brown on the bottom, about 40–45 minutes. Cool and then store in fridge in an airtight container. Can be frozen.

10. "Make new Friends"

Ten-year-old Bev stepped on to the yellow school bus quickly to get out of the cold. She grabbed a seat next to her friend Barb. They huddled together to get warm as the whole music class of fifth graders had waited for the bus outside the school a bit longer than their teacher, Mrs. Bell had expected. She had made them laugh though because they were all doing what she called the "winter shuffle", stomping their feet back and forth to try to keep their toes warm.

Soon, all thirty kids were loaded. Mrs. Bell did a head count and told the driver of the bus that they were all there and were ready to go.

The class was going to an old folks' home to sing for the residents that afternoon. Bev was always excited to sing, but was a little nervous about seeing old people. She had never had much to do with Senior Citizens. Her own grandparents were only in their late fifties.

As the bus made its way across town, the volume of noise in the bus steadily grew. Everyone was excited to be out of the classroom with an actual audience to sing for.

"Barb, what do you think the old folks will be like?" Bev asked nervously.

"Oh, Bevy, I think they will be great. My Great-Grandma lives in a home like this one and she and her friends are really fun ladies. They are always going out on excursions to the mall, or to museums or out to casinos and they ride on buses just like this to get there, except they have a ramp for those in wheelchairs."

Feeling better, Bev smiled and sat back to enjoy the ride. Soon, they were pulling up to the "Mystic Gardens" nursing home. The Driver parked the bus and then Mrs. Bell got up to give them all instructions.

"Children, listen up. We are going to line up outside the bus in our normal choir order so that we can file into our spots quickly. We must all be quiet as some residents are napping or sleeping in their rooms. We are going into the residents' living area where those that are attending are waiting for us already. Now, remember, enjoy this experience, and let the music fill your heart with joy. Don't forget to smile!"

The children all got in line, put their Santa hats on and proceeded single file into the building. Bev noticed that there was a security desk and guard on duty and that he had to buzz them all in. Once inside, she was hit immediately with an antiseptic smell. It smelled like the hospital had when she went to visit her Dad after his surgery. Her nose wrinkled up in distaste.

"Bev, this does not look like my Grandma's home at all," Barb whispered.

As they quietly walked down the hallway to the living area, they passed old people sitting in wheelchairs outside their rooms. Some smiled at them as they walked by, but most of them were just staring off into space.

Once inside the living area, Mrs. Bell instructed them to take off their coats and she piled them on a table at the side of the room. They filed into position and stared out at their audience. There were about thirty seniors in the room, some dressed in pajamas, housecoats and slippers, some dressed in street clothes. They all had big smiles on their faces. The room had tables, couches and chairs spread throughout with a TV and a piano down at the other end. Next to where they stood was a beautiful Christmas tree decorated all in red and white.

A woman in a nurse's uniform spoke with Mrs. Bell and then turned and introduced the class to the audience. The seniors clapped politely to welcome the choir.

Mrs. Bell took her place in front of them, gave them a smile and a wink of encouragement and raised her arms. Their first song was "Oh Christmas Tree", which they sung half of with the original German lyrics.

As she sang Bev let the music take over and poured her heart into her singing. She thought they sounded wonderful, as did their audience of seniors and staff, if there applause was anything to go by.

Mrs. Bell led them through each of the six songs she had selected for the day. The last song they sang was "Silent Night". As they held their last note, Bev noticed a little old lady wipe away a tear. Everyone listening to them burst into applause when they were done. That pumped up the kids and Bev knew she felt really proud of what they had just accomplished. She turned and shared a special smile with Barbie who was grinning too.

"That was wonderful, children! Thank you so much for doing your very best today. Now, each of you please go and sit with the residents and spend some time with them before we head back. Tea, juice and cookies will be served soon for everyone."

Bev tentatively walked over to the lady she had noticed crying.

"Hello. My name is Beverley," she said.

The little old lady looked up and smiled and patted the chair next to her. Bev sat down in it.

"Good day, my dear. My name is Mrs. Helen Star. I so enjoyed your singing, especially 'Silent Night'. My husband used to sing that with me. Thank you for taking the time to visit with us today. We don't get children visiting here very often."

"You are very welcome, Mrs. Star." Bev was not sure what else to say. Thankfully a staff member pushing a cart walked up to them and asked them what they would like to drink. Mrs. Star chose tea with lemon and of course Bev asked for a juice. The lady with the cart then put down a small plate of powdery, crescent shaped cookies.

"Now, tell me all about yourself, Bev," Mrs. Star said with an encouraging smile. Bev noticed that her eyes twinkled when she smiled.

Bev told her about her Mom and Dad, school, dance classes and her dogs Finnegan and Huntley, her two white Westies. They sipped their drinks and nibbled on the wonderful cookies while they chatted.

"Oh, I do miss my dogs," Mrs. Star said. "I had four Chesapeake Bay Retrievers on the farm. They were amazing dogs. What I would give to be able to have a dog with me here. I sold the farm shortly after my husband died, and of course, had to give the dogs away to a neighbour. They were definitely not city dogs. Sometimes visitors bring dogs into the home here. I love that when it happens," she said.

"Do your kids have dogs that they can bring when they visit you, Mrs. Star?" Bev asked.

"Oh, sadly enough, my dear, my husband and I were never blessed with children. I don't get any visitors anymore. My sister used to come and visit me, but she died a few years ago," she said quietly then looked away for moment.

Bev went quiet as she took a moment to think about what it must be like to not have anyone to visit you, especially at Christmas. She was surrounded by aunts and uncles and cousins at Christmas each year.

"What are you hoping that Santa brings you, Bev?" Mrs. Star asked.

"Well, I am hoping he brings me a new laptop."

"Oh, well, I don't know much about that, but you are such a good girl for coming here today, singing to us and visiting an old lady that I am sure Santa will make that happen."

Mrs. Bell then called out to the children and said it was time to go.

Bev turned to Mrs. Star and said goodbye and wished her a Merry Christmas. Mrs. Star wished her the same and patted her on the hand.

The kids all piled on the bus and the ride back to the school was a bit quieter. Again, Bev was seated next to Barb.

"I think I made a new friend today."

Bev told her all about Mrs. Star. The gentleman that Barbie had visited was equally nice.

At dinner that night Bev told her parents all about Mrs. Star and how she had no one to visit her, how she never had children and how she missed her dogs.

"Mom, Dad, can one of you please take me back to see Mrs. Star with Finnegan and Huntley before Christmas?" Bev pleaded.

Her parents smiled and said, "Of course!"

A few weeks later, on the afternoon of Christmas Eve, Bev's Mom took her and Finnegan to the nursing home. Her Mom had called ahead and made the arrangements but they were only allowed to bring one of the dogs, so her Mom suggested Finnegan because he was older and calmer.

They entered the nursing home and were told which room Mrs. Star was in. When they got to her door, they knocked and then entered. Mrs. Star was laying in her bed staring out the window. When she saw them, her face lit up.

"Oh, my dear, you don't know what this means to me!" she said, again wiping away a tear.

Her Mom introduced herself and then they gently placed Finnegan on the bed beside Mrs. Star. He sniffed her hand and then curled up alongside her. Mrs. Star petted him non-stop while they visited.

Bev gave her a poinsettia plant and a special wall calendar she had found of Chesapeake dogs. After Mrs. Star had opened it up and declared her delight with each of the twelve photos, Bev's Mom hung it up on the wall where she could see it.

"Thank you both so much for coming today. This has made my Christmas. Now, you had better get home to hang up your stocking. We can't have Santa forgetting my friend Bev now, can we?"

They hugged each other goodbye, lifted Finnegan off the bed and made their way to the door.

As they walked down the hall, Bev could hear Mrs. Star humming. It was "Silent Night", her favourite Christmas carol.

On the drive home, her Mom turned to Bev and said, "I am so proud of you, Beverley. You gave Mrs. Star the best gifts of all; your time and friendship."

The End

Mom's Almond Crescents

Mix thoroughly together ½ cup shortening and ½ cup butter. Add 1/3 cup sugar and mix in 1 package (100gms) of ground almonds. Blend together and work in 1 and 2/3 cup flour. Chill dough five minutes. Form into crescent shapes on cookie sheet. Bake at 350 degrees for 14–16 minutes. When baked roll in powdered icing sugar. These freeze well.

11. "Gifts that keep Giving"

When Lisa's Mom went to wake her that morning, Lisa said in a very hoarse voice, "Mom, I don't feel so good. My *froat* hurts."

Her Mom checked her forehead with her hand and then went to get the thermometer. When she came back from the bathroom, she said, "Put this under your tongue, and let's see what's going on here."

Lisa put the thermometer under her tongue and kept it there while her Mom kept an eye on her watch. When the time was up, her Mom took the thermometer out and read it.

"Okay, kiddo, no school for you today. Curl back up in bed, honey, and I will get you some aspirin to take this fever down a bit. Can I get you anything?"

"Some juice would be nice, Mom," Lisa whispered.

Lisa's Mom came back with a glass of apple juice and some pills that Lisa dutifully swallowed.

"Get some sleep, honey. I will check on you in a while."

Lisa didn't think she would go back to sleep, but she did and when she awoke, her Mom said her fever was better. She offered Lisa the option of moving down to the couch for the afternoon to watch TV while she did some baking.

Lisa got all settled on the couch with blankets and a mug of her favourite "sick soup", chicken noodle from the box. Her Mom turned on the Christmas tree lights for her, too. While she flipped channels she could hear her Mom in the kitchen pulling out stuff from the fridge and pantry.

"What are you making, Mom?"

"Oh, I thought I would get the Nanaimo Bars done this afternoon. I need to work on my Christmas list too, and write some more cards. You being sick, honey, ended up being a bonus day for me to get some things done around here."

"Well, glad I could help," she said with a wry grin to her Mom.

"Actually, Lisa, while I work on these bars, you can help me out in another way if you're up to it and interested. Instead of buying family members gifts they really don't need this year, your Dad and I thought we would choose gifts from this catalogue."

She grabbed a booklet from the kitchen table and brought it over to Lisa. On the cover was a picture of a smiling little black boy, holding a goat in his arms. There was also a Christmas star overlaid on top of him with the charity's name listed below in blue lettering.

"Here's the list of people we need to choose gifts for, Lisa. Why don't you go through this and choose something appropriate for each person on the list?"

With great interest, Lisa opened the booklet and saw there were so many options to choose from. Baby chicks for only $17.00, a sheep for $50.00, a goat for $75.00 or three hens and a rooster for $80.00. Flipping through the pages Lisa could see there were lots of other options too: educating a girl for a year, clean water, maternity beds, stocked pharmacies, maternal health care, school supplies, stacks of books, vegetable gardens, bed nets, birth certificates, bee-keeping kits, fuel efficient stoves, and even bathrooms for girls only.

She read about what impact each of these gifts would have on not only one child or family, but on a whole community. Some of the donations were even matched by companies that worked with this charity.

Getting excited, Lisa said, "Mom, this is an awesome idea. How much can I spend?"

Lisa's Mom laughed: "Well, what we usually spend on all those family members is about a thousand dollars, kiddo, so go nuts."

Lisa took her Mom's pad of paper and very carefully chose gifts for all her extended family members. Her Aunt Trisha was an easy choice because she was a Pharmacist, so she chose the stocked pharmacy for her. Her Grandma Mildred was a Librarian all through her life so she chose the stack of books to donate in her name. Her other Aunt and Uncle were expecting a baby so she chose the maternity bed and supplies for them. Her Uncle Don was a principal, so she chose the school essentials for him and Aunt Betty.

When it came to all her cousins, she picked the animals. Little chicks for her youngest cousin Sarah, a sheep for her brother Ben and baby pigs for her cousins Casey and Dan.

"Hey, Mom, I can't figure out what to get Uncle Dick."

Uncle Dick was her Mom's youngest brother. He was not married yet and lived in another city. They usually only got to see him once or twice a year, but she knew her Mom and Grandma were excited because he was coming home for Christmas.

Wiping her hands on a tea towel, her Mom came over and sat on the arm of the couch, peering over Lisa's shoulder as Lisa flipped through the pages.

"Hey, that goat has a beard like Uncle Dick's! Let's get him a goat, Lisa. He'll get a chuckle over that."

Lisa smiled and wrote down a goat next to Uncle Dick's name. She then added up what all of her choices cost and said, "Mom, this is just under five hundred dollars . . . is that okay?"

"Well, sweetie, why don't we educate two girls for a year through scholarships with the other five hundred dollars? Your Dad and I budgeted to donate that much and it is such a good cause. What do you think?"

Lisa eagerly wrote down educational scholarships for two girls on her list.

"Okay, Mom, all done. Now what? How do we do this?"

"Well, here . . . let me grab my laptop and you can go online and get this all ordered along with the customized gift cards they will send for each person."

It did not take Lisa long to get it all ordered and for a return email to pop up in the inbox with their charitable receipt.

"Wow, Mom, I can't believe how easy that was. That has to be the quickest Christmas shopping trip you ever made!"

"Yes, indeed, my dear. Just think of the impact the gifts you chose will have and how many lives we touched today, not only for Christmas but for years to come. Amazing! Now, how about a cup of hot tea and a Nanaimo bar, kiddo?"

Lisa and her Mom curled up on the couch and each nibbled a wonderful bar while they chose a Christmas movie to watch together for the rest of the afternoon.

The End

Mom's Nanaimo Bars

¼ cup sugar
1½ cups butter
5 tbsp. cocoa powder

Melt the above over hot water. Then add 1 beaten egg, 1 tsp. vanilla, 2 cups graham wafer crumbs and 1½ cups of chopped walnuts. Pack the mixture into an 8x8 pan.

Mix together:
2 cups icing sugar
2 tsp. Bird's Eye custard powder
Small amount of milk.

Spread over the first layer in the pan. Harden in fridge.

Melt 4 squares of semi-sweet chocolate with 1 tbsp. butter. Pour over top and spread. Keep refrigerated.

12. "Made with Love"

Oliver had just turned three years old and he was enthralled with Christmas for the first time. His Mom and Dad had set up a beautiful Christmas tree in the living room and he loved to stare at all the pretty ornaments, especially the star on top. His Mom had even let him choose two new ornaments at the store. Those were his favourites.

He wasn't sure what it was all about, but he knew someone named Santa was going to come to his house soon and there would be gifts for him to open under the tree. He was good at opening gifts, as he had demonstrated with glee at his birthday party on the weekend.

His Great Aunt had given him an ornamental little house that had bright lights on it with windows and a tiny door. Sometimes he knocked on the door to see if Santa would come out, but no luck so far.

He also liked to call the North Pole and talk to the Elves each day on his special radio that he had gotten for his birthday. Each day the Elves told him what they were working on in their workshop: bicycles, wagons, building blocks, dolls, robots and even toy dragons.

Tonight he was going to help his Mom make Christmas cards that she would send out to people who did not live in their city. He had seen cards coming to the house each day in the mailbox and liked to look at them after his Mom strung them on a ribbon on the wall behind the couch. They all had pretty pictures on them and some were sprinkled in glitter. He was excited at the thought of making such pretty cards but was not sure how they would do it.

"Oli, do you want to come choose the shapes you would like to use on the cards?" Mom asked.

He went to the dining room table and saw she was pointing to a pile of metal cookie cutters. He liked to bake cookies. He also saw two potatoes lying next to the cutters along with his paint set.

"Mom, why are you using cookie cutters for the cards and what do we need potatoes for?"

"Well, Son, once you pick the shapes you want to use I am going to cut them into half of a potato and that is what we will use to stamp the paint onto the cards," his Mom explained.

Looking at all the cutters, he studied each carefully. He chose a candy cane, a tree, a snowflake and a star from the pile of cutters.

"Those are awesome choices, Oli."

Oliver watched as his Mom then cut each potato in half and then pressed the cutter into each. She then used a sharp knife to slice around the cutter. When she was done, the potato half had the cookie cutter shape sticking up out of it.

"Okay, Oliver, now you can get creative and make some cards for us to send."

She showed him how to paint each shape sticking out of the potato and pulled a stack of blank paper cards that she had made out of his big roll of art paper. She then showed him how to stamp each card on the front with the potato and then move the card over to the side table to dry.

"Our cards won't look like the ones people have been sending to us, all shiny and bright," he said doubtfully.

"Well, Oliver, no, they won't be as shiny, but they will mean so much more because you made them with love. Too often, people are rushed at this time of year and don't have time to make their own decorations, cookies, cards or wrapping paper. Christmas is all about giving, Oliver, and making gifts yourself is a gift from the heart. You and I have lots of time though, so we can spend it making Christmas crafts ourselves."

"We can?" he asked excitedly.

"You bet! When we finish these we can cut big pieces of paper off your roll and make wrapping paper too."

Nodding his head in agreement, he turned all his attention to the task at hand. Oliver took time to decide which stamp and colour of paint to use for each card and where he would place the stamp on the front cover of the card. He chose pink for the tree, blue for the snowflake, red for the candy cane and yellow for the star. Before long, he had thirty-six cards made that were drying nicely. He thought they were beautiful.

"Okay, next step, Son, is to clear this all away and we can start writing inside the cards that are dry."

One by one, his Mom wrote inside the cards, sending warm greetings from his family and wishing everyone a Happy New Year, too. On the back of each card she wrote, "Made with Love by Oliver". When she was done writing, she let Oliver sign his name on the bottom with a red pencil crayon. His day school Teacher said he was "very advanced" in putting letters together and he could even write O-L-I. He had practiced this earlier in the week when he sent out his thank you cards to all the people that gave him birthday gifts.

His Mom then put the home-made Christmas cards into envelopes and wrote the address on the front. She let Oliver seal them and then put the postage stamp on them.

"Tomorrow, Oliver, we will walk down to the Post Office and you can put them in the mailbox so that the Mailman can deliver them to everyone, all across the country."

Once they were done with their craft for the night, Mom made him some hot chocolate and let him try a piece of the fudge she had made earlier while he took his afternoon nap. He liked it.

"Mommy, you made this fudge with love too," he declared.

"I sure did, Oliver, because I made it for you and who loves you most?" she asked with a laugh and then began to tickle him. They laughed and giggled until it was time for a story and bed.

The End

Five Minute Fudge

2/3 cup evaporated milk
1 2/3 cup sugar
½ tsp. salt
1 ½ cup (16) medium diced marshmallows
½ cup chopped nuts (I use pecans)
1 ½ cup semi-sweet chocolate chips
1 tsp. vanilla

Mix milk, sugar and salt in large, heavy saucepan. Heat to boiling, then cook for 5 minutes, stirring constantly. Begin timing the 5 minutes after mixture begins bubbling around edges of pan. Remove from heat, add marshmallows, nuts, chocolate and vanilla.

Stir fudge until marshmallows and chips are melted. Pour into an 8x8 pan. Refrigerate. Fudge is such a tricky thing to get right, but I find this one works well.

13. "Hear the snow Crunch"

Seven-year-old Karen had waited all week for Friday to arrive. Each day she had been pestering her Dad as to when they would make the annual outing to go buy the Christmas tree. Dad had said Friday night after dinner and that was in just a few hours.

Karen assumed her Dad would go to the grocery store a few blocks away because in their parking lot was a huge, beautiful tree lot with all kinds of trees. They had Christmas music playing and lots of lights strung over their massive fenced display area. They handed out hot chocolate to everyone too. Her friend Nancy, who lived four doors down, had boasted that her Dad had bought their tree there and that it was the best one on the lot. When Karen had gone to the grocery store on the weekend with her Dad, she had pointed out the huge lot wanting to grab the tree then.

Her Dad had looked over at the lot, shook his head and said, "Not today, Karen. Your Mom is not off work until Saturday, so the plan is to decorate the tree on Sunday. If we get the tree Friday night that will be soon enough for it to thaw out."

So, Friday it was. She trudged home from school in deep snow wearing her snow boots and parka. Her teacher had wrapped her scarf around her forehead and face to prevent frostbite. They were barely keeping her warm though as each time she breathed in the cold air and exhaled, her scarf got damp and was freezing to her face a bit. While it felt like a mile, thankfully, it was only a two-block walk.

Once inside the house, she kicked off her boots, unwrapped all her outerwear and hung it up on the hooks at the back door. There was a furnace vent right below that would help dry things out before she had to put them back on for their trip to the tree lot.

"Mom, I'm home," she announced.

"Oh, thank heavens. Are you frozen solid, sweetie?" her Mom asked as Karen dropped her bag on the Deacon's bench in the kitchen. Her Mom was up and writing out Christmas cards at the kitchen table, adding in a folded copy of the annual Christmas letter her Dad typed each year. Her Mom was a Nurse and worked the night shift, so Karen was never sure if she would be awake by the time she got home from school or not.

In reply Karen walked up to her Mom, gave her a hug and then laid her cold hands on her Mom's cheek.

"Eeeek!" her Mom cried out in protest. "You are as cold as an icicle!" She rubbed Karen's hands to get them warm again.

"Would you like some fairy tea to warm you up, honey?"

"Oh, yes please." Fairy tea was mostly milk with some tea and sugar added.

Karen sat with her Mom, drank her tea and ate some "And/Ors" (store bought cookies). Her Mom called them "And/Ors" because if you read the ingredients on the packaging, it usually said "may contain this ingredient and/or that ingredient". All the Christmas cookies her Mom and sisters had baked so far were frozen in the deep freeze downstairs, waiting for the Christmas Open House her Mom and Dad always held the Sunday before Christmas.

As she nibbled on a cinnamon swirl cookie, she stared at the painting above the bench in the kitchen. It was a Grandma Moses print called "Out for the Christmas Tree" and it was Karen's favourite picture they had in the house. In the picture people were cutting down trees in the forest, hauling them to their Victorian era farm homes on the back of horse drawn sleds and chopping up wood in front of their houses. It was a magical winter scene.

"What's for supper, Mom? When will Dad get home so we can go get the tree?"

"I have Swiss steak in the oven and he should be home soon. Why don't you go practice on the organ so you are ready for your lesson tomorrow morning? Your sister is not home yet because she has rehearsal after school. You can get in some practice time today. That way, you won't be fighting over the organ in the morning like you both usually do."

Karen's sister Kathy was playing the part of Scrooge in "A Christmas Carol" for the school play and she knew Mom was right in that Kathy had not practiced on the organ that week while she memorized lines.

With a big sigh Karen said, "Okay," and went into the living room to practice. She was learning a few songs from their Christmas song book this month.

Soon, her two sisters and her brother arrived home. Her Mom peeled some potatoes and set them to boil on the stove while her sister Carla made a salad. Karen and Kathy set the table while her brother Stuart watched "Hogan's Heroes" in the living room. He had wanted to watch it in the kitchen on their new colour TV but Mom said there was no point since the show was in black and white anyway. They had gotten the colour TV last year to watch the astronauts walk on the moon.

Not long after that, her Dad came in through the back door. "Hello, family," he said. "Sure smells good in here."

While they all sat down for a great dinner that warmed up their insides, they shared the highlights of their days with one another. Dessert was chocolate pudding, her brother's favourite.

Once the dishes were done, her Dad said, "Okay, who wants to go see a man about a tree?" Normally, when her Dad was leaving the house and she asked where he was going he always said, "Going to see a man about a dog."

Karen laughed and said, "I do, I do!"

"Make sure you both get bundled up," said Mom. "It's going to be a cold trip."

Karen and her Dad both put on layers of clothes and while her Mom tied her scarf for her, Dad went out to start the car to get it all toasty warm.

The air was so cold the ground crackled and crunched when you walked on it. It was a little foggy too. Nothing like the middle of December on the prairies.

Her Dad drove carefully on the slippery streets but still whistled a bit and tapped his rings on the steering wheel in time to the holiday music playing on the radio.

Karen watched with anticipation as that big tree lot came into view, but was surprised when her Dad did not turn in to it. He kept driving right by it.

"Dad, aren't we going to get the tree there?" she asked.

"No, we are definitely not buying it there. We are going to head over to Thirty-Third Street and buy it from a better lot I saw earlier."

Wow, what could be better than the lot we've just passed? Maybe they had real reindeer there like she had seen in a movie?

Finally, her Dad pulled up to a lot; well, if you could call it that. It had a small wooden shack, a rickety old sign out front saying "Christmas Trees by Klaus" and only one string of coloured lights draped around the door of the shack. There was a wooden star wrapped in white lights that hung over the door, which glowed through the foggy night.

"Dad, why is this lot better than the other one?"

"Well, Karen, I am sure that the trees are just as good there, but what makes this special is Klaus is trying to earn a living by doing this all by himself without a big grocery chain backing him. If we don't support the local guy, he might not be able to provide a great Christmas for his own family."

Sure enough, an older man came out of the shack when they got out of their car. He had a scruffy white beard and was all bundled up in an army jacket.

"Evening, folks," he said.

"Good evening to you, too. We are looking for a great tree that will make my daughter happy, Klaus. I know you can help us out."

"Oh, you bet. It would be my pleasure to find you and your daughter the perfect tree."

They walked over to the trees and Karen just saw frozen mounds, all bundled up tight like they were in their own jackets. *How could you tell what was a great tree when they weren't loose, like at the other lot?*

The tree man and her Dad focused on a pile of Spruce trees that were about seven feet tall. The sign next to the trees said "$35.00".

"Dad, how can you tell what is going to be a great tree?" Karen asked.

"Well, you look at the stem from the bottom of the tree and see if it looks like it has a straight trunk all the way up. Then, you make sure the bulk of the tree is evenly distributed as it gradually tapers off."

Finally, they found one that seemed to meet all of her Dad's criteria.

"Well, Karen, what do you think?"

"Sure, Dad, it looks great!"

The man helped her Dad load it on the roof of the car and strap it down. Her Dad then handed him a $50.00 bill and told him to "keep the change".

Klaus thanked him, shook Dad's hand and wished them both a Merry Christmas. He also pulled out a small candy-cane from his pocket and handed it to Karen.

When they got home, her Dad and her brother carried the tree into the house. Karen watched as they propped it up in the laundry room on top of some old towels and a plastic bag. Dad said that was so the tree could thaw out before they put it in the stand with a fresh cut of the trunk the next day.

Her Dad and brother then pulled the stairs to the attic down, climbed up and brought down all the Christmas ornaments. They stacked the boxes in the living room in preparation for Sunday.

Her Mom made them all hot chocolate once they were done and even pulled out some of her frozen Ginger Snaps to dunk in it.

When Karen woke up the following morning, she went to the laundry room to check on the tree; it hadn't fully thawed out, however, it was great that she could smell just a hint of the tree now.

Later that morning when Karen and her sister returned home from their organ lessons, Karen could see that her Dad had clipped off the twine that bundled the tree and it had started to fall into shape. The smell just kept getting stronger.

That evening, the tree had fallen enough for it to be placed into the big green metal stand in the living room positioned in front of the window. Karen loved that stand because it had a picture of Santa flying with his reindeer on it. Her Dad sawed off a chunk from the bottom of the tree trunk and drilled a hole up the centre of it. Stuart and her Dad then carried it into the living room and placed it in the stand, securing the three bolts that held it in place.

"Karen Faye . . . by morning it will be ready to decorate."

Karen knew that her Mom always strung the lights first and then the whole family helped add the ornaments and tinsel, finishing off with the glass blown star on top. She could not wait.

"Dad, this is going to be the best tree ever," she declared, happily. And it was indeed the perfect backdrop to yet another warm family Christmas in their home with family and friends.

The End

Mom's Swiss Steak

This is such an easy recipe, but tastes so good. Brings back a lot of memories!

One large piece of round steak. Dredge steak with mixture of flour, salt and pepper. Hammer it with kitchen mallet. Place into casserole dish with 1 large can of tomatoes and 1 can of button mushrooms. You can also add in a green pepper and an onion cubed into chunks. Dash of oregano. Bake for 3–4 hours at 300 degrees (I use my crockpot on low setting). Serve over mashed potatoes.

14. "Shoppers rush home with their Treasures"

Annie waited patiently for her Dad to answer his cell phone. It seemed to be always ringing because her Dad was a realtor.

"Darren here," he said.

They had just arrived at the big mall in the city for a father/daughter shopping day. Annie was eleven years old and had been sharing a special day at the mall with her Dad for a few years now. It was a highlight for Annie as it not only gave them some time alone, it was actually great fun to help her Dad pick out some gifts for her Mom and her little sister Maddie.

Last year they had chosen her Mom a new coffee table. The year prior, a mirror for the front entrance way and on their first trip, a wall clock for the living room. Her Mom had loved each and every gift she had helped her Dad choose. Annie was old enough to recognize that the true joy of Christmas was in the giving of gifts, not receiving them.

Her Dad loved Christmas, as did she. Her Mom preferred to shop online and was at home right now actually making the Gum Drop balls with Maddie.

While her Dad chatted with whomever was on the other end of the line, Annie surveyed the crowd. *Not too bad for a Saturday two weeks before the big day*, she thought. She liked to watch people, so she leaned on the glass railing and looked down to the first floor.

People were already lining up with their little kids to see Santa in the main courtyard. Annie could see there were two lines. One was called "Santa's Express" with a till to pre-purchase photos. They must have been expensive because there were not very many people in that line. Annie watched the process and saw that if you used the express lane you just stood for a moment until Santa was free and then an Elf lowered a red velvet rope and ushered you right in.

Her eyes focused in on a mother standing almost at the front of the other line with a toddler in a stroller and a little boy at her side. The mother had pulled out an envelope from her purse and was counting the cash inside of it. *She seemed to look a little sad and somewhat desperate*, Annie thought. The little boy at her side started pointing at something in the window of the store they were standing in front of. He looked up at his Mom and started pulling on her sleeve to get her attention. She looked over to what the boy was pointing at and then down at him and shook her head "No". The little guy burst into tears and started wailing so loudly that everyone else in the Santa line turned to look at the young family. The mother knelt down and spoke to the boy for a few moments while he stomped his feet. By the time he calmed down a little the toddler in the stroller had also started to fuss.

The man standing in front of the young mother with the kids turned to her and said something. Annie watched her reaction and then saw the woman hurry away from the line, dragging the little boy and her stroller out into the mall, all of which just increased the boys crying.

How sad, Annie thought. *That woman just left the line, in which she had no doubt been standing in for quite a while, because of that rude man.*

"Sorry, Annie, I had to take that call," her Dad said as he joined her at the railing and put his arm around her shoulder.

"That's okay, Dad. Where do you want to start?"

Her Dad named off a few stores where they could choose some toys for her little sister, as well as the main department store for her Mom's gifts.

Turning into the crowd with her Dad, Annie forgot about the woman and her family. She and her Dad were soon caught up in making some great selections in the stores they visited. The bags were adding up.

Her Dad was always great at noticing funny things. They laughed and had a grand time watching people and looking at all of the wonderful window displays as they made their way down the mall.

At one point they stopped at a fancy coffee shop. Her Dad had a coffee and she had a hot chocolate. When they were finished, they loaded up their bags once more and headed to the big department store. First they bought her Mom a bottle of her perfume, then a new purse and finally ended up in the housewares. They chose a brand new sewing machine for her Mom.

"That is going to blow her away, Dad," Annie declared. "She will absolutely love it!"

Her Dad arranged to pick it up off the dock on the back side of the store when they were done at the mall. On their way back to the main entrance they passed by the Santa's Village on the main floor.

"Annie, I know you will think this is crazy, kiddo, and you will probably say you are too old, but I want us to get a photo with Santa. Just the two of us."

Annie looked up at her Dad in surprise. *If she was too old for it, then he was WAY too old to sit on Santa's lap.* However, she could see the excitement and glee on her Dad's face.

"Well, okay, Dad, who am I to say no to the best Dad in the world?"

"Great! Then let's go buy our package for photos now and then you can just sit on that bench with the bags while I go grab one more thing."

They did just that and Annie took their receipt and went to wait on the bench. While she patiently waited for her Dad she took the time once again to observe all the activity. She listened to the excitement in the little kids' voices around her, enjoyed the Christmas music playing in the background and the jingle of the bells from the man at the donation kettle nearby. *The display is very beautiful this year*, Annie thought. They had Santa literally at the North Pole in an artic setting with an igloo as his house. The backdrop was shimmering Northern Lights that faded in and out. Above the entire scene was a huge blue and silver star hung over the igloo where Santa sat on his big chair, which was all lit up with tiny white lights. Next to Santa's chair was a giant stuffed polar bear standing on its hind legs. It was all very pretty in an icy kind of way.

She started to look around for her Dad. *Where could he be?* As she searched the crowd she saw the young mother, her son and baby approaching her as they walked by. They stopped on the other side of the bench from where she was seated and the mother seemed to collapse as she sat down. She dug out juice boxes from the back of the stroller to give the children. Annie could now see the child in the stroller was a sweet little girl.

Annie heard the mother say, "I am sorry, Kevin, but we can't see Santa today. I've spent all the extra money we had to spend and I have to save the rest for bus fare and rent. There is no way we are trying to stand in that long line again. I need to get you both home for a nap. We will come back another day to see Santa, early on a morning when the line-up is not this long, okay?"

With a quickened beat of her heart, Annie excitedly turned to the woman and said, "Excuse me for interrupting, but I have these two tickets for photos with Santa that I cannot use now. Would you like them for your little boy and girl?"

The little boy named Kevin jumped up and down in excitement and smiled at Annie.

"Are you sure you don't need these tickets?" the Mom asked.

"Yes, I am absolutely sure. Here, take these tickets and you can walk right up and be the next one to see Santa!"

Annie handed the woman the tickets that her Dad had bought. The young mother looked at Annie with a grateful smile: "God Bless you for this," she said. "You have no idea what my day has been like."

Annie thought to herself, *Oh yes I do*, but instead said, "You are most welcome. Merry Christmas."

She then saw her Dad walking up to her with more bags in his hand, one of which Annie noticed was from her favourite store.

"Oh, Annie, I'm sorry I took so long."

"No problem. Daddy, I hope you are not too disappointed but I gave our tickets away to that woman for her two kids," she said, while pointing to Kevin and his sister who were now sitting on Santa's lap.

As Annie told her Dad the whole story, they watched the photographer take the photo. Little Kevin was grinning from ear to ear and his little sister was staring up at the strange man in the red suit with a questioning look.

"I am so proud of you, Annie, for the decision you just made. You are the BEST daughter in the whole world and while I would have loved a goofy photo of us together with the 'Big Red Dude', we can always get one another time. Now, why don't we head home to Mom and Maddie and see if they have some gumdrop balls ready for us?"

Together they turned and walked away and out into the cold, winter air, parcels in hand and with the spirit of Christmas in their hearts.

The End

Gum Drop Balls

One of my favourites. Messy to make, but worth it!

1 can sweetened condensed milk
3 cups of cornflakes crushed (measure before crushing)
1 tsp. almond extract
Pinch of salt
1 cup baking gum drops, cut fine (this takes a while to do and I just use a scissors to cut into quarters)
½ cup crushed nuts (I use pecans)
Coconut

Heat milk and add salt in a double boiler until it begins to thicken for approximately 10 minutes. Allow to cool slightly. Add cornflakes, nuts, gum drops and vanilla. Let stand 15 minutes. Make into small balls (this is the extremely messy part). Then roll them in coconut. These freeze well but I prefer to just refrigerate them so this is one of the last recipes I make each year. They disappear really quickly!

15. "Simple and Sweet"

Little six-year-old Carla was gently awoken with the cool touch of her mother's hand on her cheek.

"Honey, Mom has to go to work now. Auntie Erna is in the kitchen having a cup of coffee. She is going to babysit you today, okay? I want you to be a very good girl and do as you're told for Auntie."

Carla rubbed her eyes and sat up to give her Mom a hug goodbye. "Have a good day at work, Mom."

"Thanks, honey. I will. You have fun today too with Auntie."

Her Mom got up from the edge of her bed and then made her way out the bedroom door and down the hall. Carla knew it was really early because her Mom left for work at the Hospital before the sun was even up. She laid back down and drifted off to sleep again.

When she next awoke the sun was drifting in through her bedroom window. She sprang from her bed in search of her favourite Auntie and found her reading in the living room on the couch.

"Good Morning, Auntie," she chirped as she launched herself on to her Aunt's lap.

"Well, good morning to you too my sleeping beauty. I was just waiting for you to wake up peanut. Why don't we get you some breakfast?"

Together they went to the kitchen and Auntie dished up a bowl of porridge that Mom had made in the double boiler before she left.

After pouring on some milk and brown sugar, Carla dug in to her hot, sweet porridge. Her Auntie sat down with her with a fresh cup of coffee and some cinnamon toast to share.

"Did you see our tree, Auntie? It's not done yet though."

That summer, Carla and her Mom had been evacuated from their home and all their things that were in the house had been lost. They would never be able to go back to their home because the town had condemned it after a massive flood. Carla and her Mom were lucky to have found this apartment to move into and each week Mom had slowly been buying new things; first beds for them to sleep in, then a kitchen table and chairs, then pots and pans and things for the kitchen. Carla's Grandma had sent them lots of care packages with clothes, and in the last package had been two new Christmas stockings. They, along with the tree, were the only Christmas decorations they had in the house.

"Yes, honey, I saw. I've been sitting next to it reading and enjoying the fresh pine smell and the pretty lights. It is a beautiful tree."

"Auntie, it looks scraggly; there are no ornaments on it. We lost them all when we were 'disastered' in the summer and Mommy said she has to wait until her next payday to buy some more."

"Well, Carla, first and foremost you have to enjoy the beauty of the tree. The ornaments are just dressing on top. Kind of like how you love the person first . . . not what they are wearing. You love me, not these beads I have around my neck, right?"

Carla nibbled on her toast and thought about that.

"Carla, I just had a thought; how would you like to surprise your Mom and have the tree all decorated by the time she gets home?"

"Really? How will we pay for the ornaments at the store though, Auntie? I don't have any of my allowance left."

Auntie laughed: "We don't need money to decorate that tree, Carla."

"We don't?"

"No, we don't. Why don't we bake some cookies to hang on the tree and then string some popcorn for the garland today? The only thing we need to go to the store for is a bag of fresh cranberries."

Excited, Carla nodded in eager agreement. That sounded like a very fun way to spend a Sunday.

After they were done with breakfast and washed up the few dishes, Carla got dressed and they left the apartment to walk to the corner grocery store for the cranberries. Auntie also bought some sprinkles and icing for the cookies. It was getting colder outside but the sun was still shining, making the snow glimmer.

"Auntie, what are we going to put on the top of the tree? We used to have a star that plugged into the lights."

"Hmmm, let me think about that for a minute, peanut. I am sure we can come up with something. You know, Carla, while Christmas may never be exactly the same because you lost your decorations, it can still be just as special. You can create new memories with your Mom in this new home and I know that Santa has your new address."

When they returned home, Auntie pulled out her sister's recipe book and found the recipe for the Christmas Tree Cookies that Carla's Mom usually made. They were spicy and crisp and Carla loved them. Soon the batter was made and they were rolling out cookies. Auntie let her cut the shapes and then, before she put them in the oven, she used a straw to cut a hole in the top of each cookie. She explained to Carla that that was where they would slip the thread through so they could hang them on the tree.

When the cookies were all baked, iced and decorated, they cut some thread and then tied the cookies to the tree. They looked really good and tasted even better.

"Okay, kiddo. Next thing we have to tackle is the garland. Let's have some soup for lunch first and then we can pop the corn."

Once the corn was popped, Auntie doubled up some thread on a needle and showed Carla how to pierce each piece of popcorn, followed by a cranberry, then another piece of popcorn. While they strung the pieces Auntie asked her about which toys Carla missed the most and what she hoped Santa would bring her that year.

After a couple of hours they had eight whole strands of garland done, which they placed on the tree. It looked beautiful now.

"Carla, I think I have a plan for the star on top. You are right in that every tree has to have a star on top. I think if we take this empty toilet paper role and cover it in tin foil, we can add a paper star to it cut from a paper plate."

Auntie pulled out a paper plate that they still had from when they had no dishes and drew a star on it, which Carla then cut out with her own set of "safe" scissors. Then they wrapped it in tinfoil. Auntie taped it onto the holder and then wrapped that in foil too. When it was finished, Auntie stood on a chair and placed the star on top of the tree. It was perfect.

"Oh, Auntie, Mom is going to be so surprised and happy when she sees the tree."

"Yes, I am sure she will be, Carla. Now, nap time for you missy while I get supper started. Then we can eat when your Mom gets home and tonight, we can light the Third Advent candle together before I head home."

When Carla awoke from her nap, spaghetti sauce was simmering on the stove and Auntie had the pasta water boiling too in preparation for her Mom's arrival.

It was not long before Carla heard the key in the door.

"Mom, Mom, you won't believe what we did today! Come and see the tree!"

When Carla's Mom came into the living room and saw the tree, she broke down and cried, hugging Carla and then her sister Erna.

"Oh my, what would I do without my two special Santas?" she said. "You have made me believe that Christmas will be better than just okay this year and that life will get back to normal once more. Thank you both so much for all the hard work you did today."

The three of them sat down for a yummy dinner and Carla told her Mom all about their day of activities, including how they made the star for the tree.

When they were done eating dinner, they all gathered around the tree and Mom lit a candle for the Advent. It was indeed going to be a very simple and sweet, special Christmas after all.

The End

Christmas Tree Cookies

I have been making these cookies since I was old enough to bake on my own. They are a perfect cookie to roll and cut, making a nice alternative to the sugar cookies on your goodie tray.

2½ cups flour
2 tsp. baking soda
2 tsp. cinnamon
2 tsp. cloves
2 tsp. ginger
1 ½ cups sugar
1 cup butter or margarine
1 egg
2 tbsp. corn syrup

Mix flour, soda and spices together. Cream butter, sugar and egg thoroughly. Add corn syrup and blend. Add the flour mixture gradually. Mix well. Chill 1 hour or until firm. Roll to 1/8 inch thickness, cut and place on greased baking sheets. Sprinkle with decorations. Bake at 400 degrees for 5–8 minutes. Yields 3–4 dozen cookies.

16. "Sew this is Christmas"

Trisha trudged home from school with a determined step. She had a "to-do" list longer than most adults, which was not unusual for this twelve-year-old. Circumstances had thrown her into adulthood far sooner than was normal. She had a sick mother and two little sisters to care for while her Dad tried to keep his business above water.

Above water. That was ironic considering her Dad's flower shop had been wiped out in the flood earlier that year. The re-opening had just been two weeks ago, but business was slow to bounce back. She could see the unspoken worry in her Dad's eyes and demeanour whenever he thought no one was watching. He tried to keep up appearances that all was "okey dokey" with her Mom and the younger kids, but Trisha knew he was very worried about their financial security. Normally, this was her Dad's best season with people buying poinsettia plants, ornate arrangements of cut flowers and greenery to decorate their houses with.

Unfortunately, most people in town were still rebuilding their homes and flowers were not high on their list of priorities this year. If business did not pick up for Christmas, Trisha knew January would be devastating financially. It was a long way until Valentine's Day, which was their biggest day of the year for flower sales.

The truth was though that the flower shop had not been the same since her Mom got sick. Mom was a creative genius and had been the driving force that set them apart from every other flower shop in town. *Actually,* Trisha thought, *nothing has been the same since Mom was diagnosed with Multiple Sclerosis.*

Shaking off the depressing thoughts, she quickened her step to get home. She had to prepare dinner, help her sisters with their homework, do her own homework and then hopefully have enough time to start her special project tonight.

Trisha loved to sew. Her Mom had taught her at a very young age and together they had made many beautiful things. She loved selecting the fabric and then working with the material to first cut and then sew something into a beautiful finished project.

This year, her Christmas gift to her family members was going to be new stockings to hang up on Christmas Eve. She had chosen varying tones of blue velvet for the main part of the stockings and then a gorgeous patterned piece of white material to form the cuffs. She was not sure what she was going to line the stockings with yet, but knew her Mom had a bunch of fabric in her craft room that she could choose from. She had even bought little silver metal stars to hang off the points of the cuffs. She knew they were going to look beautiful; however, the problem was just finding the time to get them made.

She had thought she would get them done this past weekend, but her Dad had asked her to work in the shop so that he could give Mary, his main worker, some time off. Trisha realized that her Dad was trying to keep his labour costs down as much as he could. So, like always, Trisha had agreed to help him out, especially as her Aunt had been willing to come over to watch the girls and her Mom.

Entering in through the front door of their home, Trisha set her book bag down and went in to greet her Mom. Kari, the nurse that came in every weekday was only there until 6pm, so Trisha had two hours to get her to-do list done before her Dad would be home for dinner.

"Hi, Mom. How was your day?" Trisha asked, as she bent over the special hospital bed they had set up in what used to be her Mom's office on the main floor. She kissed her Mom hello, saw a smile in her eyes and then turned to Kari to get an update.

"Oh, we had a great day, Trisha. Your Mom and I tackled the Whipped Shortbread recipe that was on the counter and got them baked."

"You did? Wow, thanks, Kari. That is awesome!" Trisha mentally ticked one more thing off her list.

Trisha sat down in her Mom's wheelchair next to the bed and told her about her day. Her Mom was having trouble speaking now so it was pretty much a one sided conversation, however, Trisha could tell she was following her story despite looking tired.

Winding down her visit she said, "Okay, well I better get started on supper. The girls will be home soon."

Sure enough, she heard the back door slam and Janey and Gabi's voices could be heard in the kitchen.

The two little devils, as Trisha thought of them most of the time, raced into her Mom's room. Janey was eight and Gabi was seven and all they seemed to do was bicker with one another.

"Mom, Janey pushed me on the ice today at recess and I fell and hurt my leg," Gabi complained.

"I did not!" was Janey's quick reply.

Trisha could see where this was going.

"Okay, you two, give Mom some hugs and then you need to get started on your homework," Trisha said.

"No, we don't. I want to stay with Mom for a while," Janey said.

Kari chimed in, "Actually, ladies, Trisha is right. Let's give your Mom some time to rest before dinner. She's quite tired."

With a dramatic sigh, they agreed and the three girls left the room to head to the kitchen.

"Oh, yummy. Shortbread," Gabi declared with delight when she saw the cookies on the counter.

"Just one each, girls. We need to save these for next week."

"Why? Christmas is just a week away; if we eat them all you can just make more," Gabi said.

Trying to reason with them, Trisha said, "I may not have time to make more and you want to be sure to have some to leave for Santa, don't you?"

"Yes," they agreed.

They each ate one cookie and then Trisha packed them away in a container and placed them in the freezer. She noticed that Kari had cleaned up all the dishes today too, so she had a clean slate to start making supper.

Her sisters grabbed their backpacks, pulled out their homework and sat at the kitchen table to get their work done. Trisha grabbed the frozen lasagna from the freezer and popped it into the oven, made the salad, and then finally sat down to tackle her own homework.

When they were all done, the younger girls raced to the living room to watch TV and Trisha set the table for dinner.

Kari came in to the kitchen to say goodnight before she left for home.

"She is sleeping now, Trisha. Tell your Dad that she will probably sleep for the rest of the night. I doubt she will join you for dinner tonight though. She had a big lunch at about two o'clock, so she should be good."

Trisha thanked Kari again for making the cookies and wished her goodnight.

So far, so good, Trisha thought. *Maybe I will have time tonight to get the stockings made.*

Just then she heard arguing in the living room. She walked in to a full blown fight between her sisters. What it was over she could not imagine.

"Girls. Mom is trying to sleep. Stop yelling right now."

Turning to her with an expression of anger she had not seen before, Janey yelled, "Stop telling me what to do, Trisha! You are not my Mom. I hate you!"

Gabi joined in and said: "Yeah, I hate you, too! You act all bossy all the time and never play with us anymore."

That was the final straw.

"Play? I don't have TIME to play because all I do is take care of you two!" Trisha burst into tears and ran to her room where she proceeded to cry her eyes out face down on her bed.

Not long afterwards, there was a gentle knock at the door.

"Trisha, can I come in," her Dad asked?

Sniffling back her sobs, she said, "Yes, Dad."

Her Dad came in and sat on the edge of the bed, rubbing her back. "Oh, pet, it breaks my heart to see you cry. What happened?"

"The girls hate me, Dad!"

"Oh, they may have said that, Trisha, but you know deep down they love you more than anything. They are just acting out because their whole world has shifted and you, my dear, are the closest target. I know your needs are always the last to be considered, Trisha, and I have spoken to the girls about respecting you. This family is in a crisis mode, but you and I both know it is only going to get more challenging. We all have to work together as a team and the girls have to help you every day, not hinder you. Now, what can I do to help?"

"Dad, more than anything I just want some time to myself so I can get to my Christmas sewing project. Time is running out and I need to get things made or I won't have gifts for any of you."

"Okay, I can make that happen. I see your Mom is sleeping soundly so here's a thought; why don't we all go eat the wonderful supper you made that smells so good and then I can take the girls out to the mall for a couple of hours tonight? I want to see what the florist there is doing in his windows anyway. Our shop was quite busy today and I need to make sure what we are offering is better than the competition."

"Really, Dad? That would be awesome! Mom will be fine tonight because Kari said she should sleep right through the night."

"Okay, then we have a plan. Dry your eyes and let's go join those monkeys in the kitchen for dinner."

They walked arm in arm into the kitchen.

"We're sorry, Trisha, we don't hate you. We love you!" the girls each declared as they each gave her a big hug.

As they sat eating their dinner, her Dad explained: "You know, girls, we all have to learn to be a little easier on ourselves. None of us can fill Mom's shoes on our own . . . all any of us can hope to do is to ensure we maintain the love amongst us so that we can be a really strong team to get us through the challenges ahead. If supper doesn't get made on time, no big deal. If the dishes don't get done in the morning, the world is not going to end. Let's try to respect one another though and recognize that we all have a role to play in this family. Christmas is a very special time of year with lots of pressure, but it will be what it will be. As long as we are all together, in our home, it will be a very special day!"

When they were done eating, Dad, Janey and Gabi did the dishes and shooed Trisha out of the kitchen into her Mom's craft room.

A great inner calm and peace came over Trisha as she set to work cutting out five stockings. She chose her matching thread and started to create something beautiful.

She remembered her Mom saying once that, "Even when God challenges us, there is beauty and grace to be found within and around you. Always look for the silver lining, Trisha, and you will find it."

With sudden inspiration, Trisha knew what fabric to line the stockings with; a beautiful silver satin that her Mom had saved from an old housecoat of hers. Trisha sewed the pieces together and as she did so, she felt a great calm come over her. Dad was right, things may not be like they once were, but they could still be good in a new way.

The End

Auntie Betty's Whipped Shortbread

A real easy, quick shortbread. Dropped by spoon or can be used in a cookie press.

1 cup butter
1½ cups of flour
½ cup icing sugar
¼ cup cornstarch
Sprinkle decorations

Cream butter and sugar. Add flour and cornstarch gradually while whipping with an electric beater. Drop on ungreased cookie sheet, add your decorations and bake for 20 minutes at 325 degrees.

17. "Naughty or Nice?"

Twelve-year-old Bobby could not believe his luck. After a family trip to the dentist this afternoon, where they had all received perfect check-ups, his Mom was driving his little sister Marcia and him home. Not only had they gotten to eat at his favourite burger joint for lunch after his Mom picked them up from school, they also did not have to go back to classes for the rest of the day.

"Now, kids, you two have a choice to make. You can stay at home and try not to kill each other, or you can come with me over to Grandma's. She wants me to stop by and help her with the Cape Breton Pork Pies. You know since her arthritis set in, she can't use her thumbs too much."

"Oh, I love pork pies," Marcia chimed in from the back seat.

Bobby did not care for them himself because he found them too sweet. For a long time he could not figure out why they were called "pork pies" when there was no meat in them at all.

They were tarts filled with dates and topped with a dollop of maple flavoured icing. Everyone raved about his Grandma's pork pies, but he was not all that keen on sweets. He preferred salty things. His Dad called him "The Chip King!" He could easily eat a whole bag himself.

"I think I will just hang out at the house, Mom," he decided.

Surprisingly, Marcia said, "Me too!" Normally, she loved going to Grandma's house.

Marcia was just nine and while he loved her as a little sister most of the time, she could be really annoying. She was always bugging him to play with her.

"Well, okay, Marcia, but if you stay at home, Bobby is in charge and you have to listen to him, understood? And Bobby, please keep an eye on your sister. You have Grandma's number in case you need me."

Mom pulled in to the driveway, waited until they had made it into the house through the garage and they had both waved to her from the living room window before she drove off again.

Bobby and Marcia kicked off their shoes and dropped their school bags. Bobby flopped on to the couch and grabbed the remote. *Hmm, what can I watch?* He flipped through the channels and found that there was nothing but soap operas and talk shows on.

"This sucks! There is nothing on TV at this time of day."

"I'm going to go play with my doll house," Marcia said. "Do you want to play with me, Bobby?"

"No, I do not want to play with you," he said.

Marcia shrugged her shoulders and headed to her bedroom.

Bobby was bored, which surprised him. He wandered around the house for a bit, grabbed a snack and checked out the presents under the tree. There were only seven for him and ten for Marcia. In disgust, he decided to head outside to shoot some pucks with his friends.

"Marcia, I'm going outside," he yelled to her.

He grabbed his net from the garage and then set it up in front of the garage. He grabbed his stick and his bucket of pucks. They were frozen solid. Perfect for some "hot shots".

He turned to go ring the doorbells of his buddies on the street, but stopped cold halfway down the driveway with the sudden realization that they were all still in school.

Shoot! He needed a goalie. He ran back inside the house.

"Marcia, come here. You have to come outside with me now," he declared in an authoritative voice.

Marcia came to the top of the landing and looked down at him. "Why?" she asked.

"Because I said so. Mom said you had to listen to me, right?"

"Yes, but I really don't want to go outside right now. It's cold!"

Turning his charm power up full notch, he said, "It will be fun! We never get to play hockey together. You're always wanting to play with me, right?"

"Well, yeah."

"Okay, so grab your coat and boots and throw on a toque and get outside."

"Okay, Bobby." Marcia was just happy to get to play with her big brother.

Once outside, Bobby told her where to stand and how to use his goalie stick. He told her to just "block any shots that came at her".

He grabbed his stick and the bucket of frozen pucks and headed halfway down the driveway.

Bobby dumped out a pile of his pucks, lined them up with his stick and started to fire shots at the net.

When the first puck whizzed by her face, Marcia's face froze into one of terror. She started to jump out of the way as her brother kept firing them at the net behind her.

"Don't be a baby! Stand in the net and try to block them, Marcia," Bobby instructed.

She tried holding the stick properly to deflect his next shot. Thankfully, most of them were wide of the net.

Growing frustrated, Bobby collected the pucks from behind the net and headed back down the driveway, but moved his shooting line closer to the net. He was determined to "score".

Just as he was winding up to shoot, he heard a car pulling up. He fired and the puck was dead on target. Unfortunately though, Marcia, having seen the car pulling up, dropped her stick and ran to greet their Mom and moved to the left. "SMACK!"

He hit her right in the face. He stared in disbelief as she started balling and clutching her face.

Her Mom leaped out of the van and ran to Marcia, "Oh my heaven, honey, let me see." She pried Marcia's hands away from her face.

"Marcia, there is no blood, I know it hurts, honey, but you're okay." She grabbed Marcia up in her arms and carried her into the house, stopping to throw Bobby one of her killer looks, the kind that said, *I am so disappointed in you.*

"Bobby, what were you thinking? Clean up this mess right away and then go to your room. Just wait until your Dad gets home."

Wounded beyond belief and still rattled from seeing the puck hit Marcia's face, he gathered up his gear, stored it in the garage and headed to his bedroom very quietly.

As he lay on his bed waiting to be called down for dinner, he thought about what had happened. He felt so bad for his little sister. He had not meant to hurt her, really. Or, had he?

Had he been so mad at her for having more gifts under the tree than him? He didn't like to think that he would take something like that out on Marcia. She had nothing to do with how many gifts she got, did she? He thought about that until he heard his Dad come in.

Not long afterwards, his parents called him down to dinner.

Walking into the kitchen, he saw Marcia sitting at the table with a bag of frozen peas pressed to her cheek.

"Hey, Bobby, guess what? I'm going to have a black eye for Christmas."

"I'm sorry about that, Marcia. I didn't mean to hit you."

He sat down and they all had a very quiet dinner. When they were done, Dad suggested to Mom that she take Marcia up for a bath and that he and Bobby would do the dishes.

As they worked together clearing the table, his Dad said, "You know, Son, your Mom and I are really disappointed in the lack of judgment you showed today. We expect more of you, especially when it comes to looking out for your sister. I shudder when I think of what could have happened, Bobby. She could have lost an eye or her teeth, or been knocked unconscious."

"I know, Dad. I would give anything if I could take it back. I was not aiming for her directly, but she moved when Mom pulled up."

"Bobby, whether it was an accident or not, you should never have put a girl in harm's way like that. If there is one thing you need to learn from us as your parents, Son, it is to always respect women and girls. That not only means how you treat them but also how you speak to them. Now, please tell me what was going on to have led you to the decisions you made."

Bobby told his Dad about his happiness at being able to stay home after the dentist and then his boredom. He also shared about how he felt after counting the gifts under the tree. He was ashamed when he told his Dad that part, but his Dad did not react, he just listened.

"Okay, well I appreciate your honesty, Bobby. Why don't you head up for your bath now, too? It sounds like Marcia is done in the bathroom."

Bobby trudged up the stairs only feeling a little better for having shared his feelings and thoughts with his Dad.

When he got out of the tub and came back downstairs, he found his Mom and Dad cuddled up on the couch with Marcia, whose cheek was getting really shiny and purplish now.

His Mom opened her arms and he climbed on to her lap. Once he was settled in nicely all snuggled up he looked over at the Christmas tree and noticed that there were only his sister's gifts under the tree now.

He looked questioningly at his Dad. *Where are my gifts?*

"Bobby, there is a week before Christmas. Mom and I have decided that you will have to earn your gifts back over the next week. Each day, when you and Marcia get home from school you will play with her for an hour doing what she wants to do. If you do that and respect her wishes, you will get a gift placed back under the tree each day."

Bobby nodded in understanding.

"We have also explained to Marcia that she should never do anything that she does not want to do just because someone tells her to do it; unless it directly concerns her safety or she is being asked to do it by a trusted adult."

"Now, are you both okay with all that?" Mom asked.

"You bet! Bobby, tomorrow will you play dolls with me?"

"Sure, Sis, whatever you want to do is fine by me!"

They all sat together for a while after that admiring the Christmas tree. Bobby thought the star on top seemed to be shining as bright as his sister's cheek.

The End

Cape Breton Pork Pies

Tart shells:
    2 cups flour
    2 tbsp. icing sugar
    1 cup butter, softened

Filling:
    2¼ cups chopped pitted dates
    1 cup water
    ¾ cup brown sugar
    ¼ tsp. salt
    1 tsp. vanilla extract

Icing:
    ¼ cup butter
    2¼ cup icing sugar
    2 tbsp. milk
    1 tsp. maple extract

Preheat oven to 325 degrees. Sift together the flour and icing sugar in a bowl. Cut in the butter and blend in like you would with pastry. Form dough into ¾ inch balls. Press a small indent evenly with your thumb into each and place into half-inch tart trays. Make sure the dough goes up the side of the cups to form a shell. Does not have to be very deep. Fill each cup with date mixture and bake until shells are golden brown. Cool and then use decorator tip to add a dollop of the maple icing on each. Refrigerate or freeze.

18. "Santa does see Everything!"

It was only a week before Christmas Day and ten-year-old Kathleen hurried home after school to see if there were any presents under the tree yet.

Her Mom was a nurse who worked the night shift so she used the time in the afternoon after she woke up to get her Christmas tasks done while Kathleen and her three siblings were still in school.

She had seen her Mom and Dad arrive home with shopping bags intermittently over the last few weeks, so she knew there were gifts in the house to be wrapped. While she knew it was wrong to peek at her gifts, she just could not seem to wait until Christmas Day to see what her parents were buying her. *It was so hard not to!*

One day last Christmas, when she thought her Mom was still sleeping, she had lain down in front of the tree. Very quietly she had taken each gift that had a tag with her name on it, and ever so gently, she had pried open the end of the package by carefully removing the tape, inch by inch.

Her little sister Karen had watched her do this and warned her, "You are going to get in trouble!"

Sure enough, her Mom walked into the living room and had caught her red-handed. Her Mom had berated her and when her Dad was told that night he had just given her that "I'm disappointed in you" look that could kill.

As her Mom had said, in the end, "All she did was ruin her own Christmas because the only surprises were the gifts that Santa had left for her unwrapped under the tree."

As she walked home, she promised herself, "I will not peek, I will not peek!"

When she walked through the back door her Mom was in the kitchen taking some Mincemeat Cookies out of the oven. They were one of Kathy's favourites.

"Hi, Mom. Those smell so good."

"Hello, my dear. Did you see Karen on your way home?"

"Yeah, she was walking with Nancy, so she is probably over there right now playing."

"Okay, I will call Louella if she is not home soon. Do you have any homework?"

"Not today; I'm going to watch TV before Stu gets home and takes takes over the TV."

She headed into the living room and immediately, her eyes were drawn to the tree. Sure enough, there were presents under it now!

She sat down in front of it and picked up each gift to shake it, smell it and most importantly, check out who it belonged to.

The first gift she picked up had no tag. Thinking it must have fallen off, she picked up another to inspect it. Nothing there either. *What is going on?* she thought.

Her Mom walked in with a big grin on her face and a small plate of cookies in hand.

"Fixed your wagon, now didn't I?" Mom asked.

"I don't understand, Mom? Why are there no names on all these presents?"

"Well, to stop any 'Nosey Parkers', this year I have coordinated all the wrap with a secret code that only I know. None of you kids will know which gifts are yours until Christmas morning so that you don't ruin your own Christmas again."

She set the cookies down on the coffee table and left Kathleen to ponder this whole new scenario. A little miffed, she sat down to watch TV.

Over the next few days, gifts arrived for the family from her Grandparents, her Aunts and Uncles. If one was for Kathleen, her Mom took the gift and locked it up in her parent's bedroom.

Finally, it was Christmas Eve. Kathleen was so excited. She could not wait for the morning to come. All that day she and her little sister had discussed what they hoped was under the tree for each of them, and what Santa would leave, too.

As was custom, her Mom made her shortbread cookies on Christmas Eve and they dutifully left a plate with both versions on it for Santa; ones with red cherries and ones with green cherries on top. Better to leave both kinds because you never knew which one Santa preferred.

Kathleen was the first to awake at 5am on Christmas Day. She banged on her siblings' bedroom doors, "Wake up! Wake up! It's Christmas!" she shouted with glee.

Her parents made them line up in the hallway in order of age, youngest to oldest. Her Dad was in the living room with his camera so he could take a picture of each of them as they walked in and saw what Santa had left for them under the tree.

First Karen, then Kathleen, then Stuart and finally Carla.

When Kathleen walked into the living room she saw that Santa had left her the board game "Clue". She could not wait to play it later in the day. She looked on the back of the gold coloured box and saw that there were characters in the game: Mrs. Peacock, Colonel Mustard, Miss Scarlet, Professor Plum, Mrs. White and Mr. Green. What fun this would be trying to solve a murder. Next to the "Clue" game was a giant gingerbread man from Santa with a note that said:

Dearest Kathleen,

Since you love to snoop, I thought you would enjoy this game of investigation. Don't forget . . . I see everything my little, "Inspector Clouseau".

Love,
Santa

Kathleen checked out what Santa had brought everyone else and looked to see if they had received any special notes. Karen got a doll, her brother got a new hockey stick and her older sister Carla, got a set of steam hair curlers from Santa, but none of them got notes from him.

Next the family did their stockings, emptying out everything inside with glee to get to the Christmas orange in the toe. Again, Santa had carried on with the investigative theme: a new Nancy Drew book, a magnifying glass, a little stuffed pink panther and a little notebook with a slot for a pencil.

Once they were done eating their oranges and Mom and Dad had refilled their coffee cups and put the breakfast meat into the oven, they came back to open the other gifts. First Mom handed Kathy and her siblings the gifts from their Grandparents, Aunts and Uncles. She received some lovely things.

Then it was time for Mom to hand out those gifts with no tags.

Kathleen watched her Mom with great anticipation, however, her Mom paused in front of the tree with a puzzled look on her face.

"Oh, Ray, I can't remember whose wrapping paper is whose?" They all laughed. She took one gift with each of the four different wrapping papers into the kitchen to open a corner on each. Once she saw what was inside, she had her secret code figured out.

"Okay, kids. Carla, your gifts are those with bells on them. Stuart, you have the ones with snowmen on them. Kathleen, yours are the ones with stars, and Karen your gifts all have Santa on them.

For an hour they opened gifts. Kathleen was joyfully surprised at each and every one of her gifts. *Mom and Dad were right,* she thought. This was such a better Christmas than last year when she had peeked.

When they had picked up all the gift wrap and placed it into a garbage bag, they sat down for their traditional Christmas breakfast: Scrambled eggs, bacon, farmer sausage, blood sausage and cornbread.

Later that afternoon, with the turkey making the house smell wonderful, the whole family played "Clue". Kathleen thought it was the greatest game ever.

The End

Mincemeat Cookies

½ cup butter
½ cup shortening
1 cup sugar
½ cup brown sugar
2 eggs
1 tsp. vanilla
3 cups flour
1 tsp. soda
1 jar (8oz) of brandied mincemeat, drained.

Cream butter, shortening and sugars. Add eggs and vanilla. Beat well. Sift flour and soda together and add to creamed mixture. Chill at least 2 hours. Form into balls slightly larger than walnuts and place on greased cookie sheet. Indent the centre with the back of a teaspoon and fill with mincemeat. Bake at 375 degrees for 12–15 minutes. Remove from pan at once to cool on rack. These are delicious!

19. "Love thy Neighbour"

When little seven-year-old Logan left the school that Thursday before Christmas he saw his Mom waiting in the van. He knew she would say that he was "dilly dallying" again, but really, his zipper had got stuck and it took him quite a while to get the jammed material out of the zipper track. It was his favourite coat but it was really getting too small for him now. He had a brand new one at home that his Grandma had bought for him, but he just loved this old one.

When he got to the van, he climbed in through the side door and jumped into his booster chair. He was not quite tall enough yet to go without it.

"Hi, Mom!"

"Hi, honey. Buckle up, Logan . . . I want to get to the grocery store before it gets crazy with after work shoppers."

His Mom had told him that they would be going shopping after school today because she "did not want to spend her last weekend before the big day fighting over frozen turkeys with other people". That had made him laugh; he had never seen shoppers fighting over food before.

Soon, they were pulling into their usual grocery store lot and already, parking was getting scarce. Finally, his Mom found a spot to pull the van into.

When they got into the front of the store, his Mom grabbed two carts instead of one.

"Logan, I need you to push a cart today too, okay?"

"Mom, are we really going to buy that much stuff for our Christmas dinner?" he asked in disbelief.

She laughed: "Well, we are not just buying groceries for our family tonight, we are also buying groceries for the family that we are filling a Christmas Hamper for with the 'Secret Santa' program."

Logan had forgot about that. He had been with his Mom when they had chosen an envelope off the tree at their Church last week. In each envelope were the first names of the family members, their age, size, and a list of items that each family member was in need of for Christmas. Along with buying them some items off their wish list, they were to provide groceries for a Christmas dinner for that family.

When they had it all purchased with gifts wrapped and labelled with the names, they were to drop it all off at the Church in a plastic bin they had been provided with. Church volunteers would see they were delivered to the family right away to ensure frozen foods stayed frozen and the other fresh food did not go bad.

Putting her purse in the front section of the first cart, his Mom turned to him and gave him the family's list she had in her hand.

"Here, honey, why don't you look after their list and I will keep ours with me?"

Logan opened up the folded paper and read:

Dad, "Alvin", age 32, size Large

Needs: Diapers, Baby Formula
Wish List: Christmas Cards and Stamps

Son, "Padget", age 6, size six

Needs: Clothes
Wish list: Lego or Books

Daughter, Roxanne, age 1, size 18months

Needs: A Mom, Clothes
Wish List: Doll

He saw that whomever had filled out the form had first written the words "A Mom" for little Roxanne's needs, then crossed it out and written clothes instead.

"Hey, Mom, why doesn't this family have a Mom? And who wishes for a box of Christmas cards?"

"All the Church office would tell me, Logan, was that the Mom was not with them anymore. I don't know if that means she died or if the Dad just has custody of his kids. I asked about the cards too and apparently the father is from down east and just really wants to be able to reach out to his family."

"If we buy him cards though, Mom, they won't get to his family in time," Logan pointed out.

His Mom stopped in her tracks and turned to him.

"Oh, Logan, I never thought of that. What are we going to get this poor man instead now? Well, let's think on that as we get the other gifts, then the food. Maybe something will come to us."

They first went to the toy department and picked out two age appropriate dolls, some books and a great Lego set that Logan would have loved for himself. Then into the clothing department where his Mom picked out baby clothes along with a big box of diapers and a case of formula. She let him choose pants, shirts, sweaters, socks and underwear for the boy. They chose a sweater for the Dad since he had not really asked for anything for himself.

Mom even insisted on buying three new Christmas stockings for them to hang. She also bought lots of chocolates and candies.

When they headed to the food section of the giant store, they wound their way through the aisles adding into each cart: a box of Christmas oranges, apples, pears, onions, celery, lettuce, Brussels sprouts, carrots, potatoes and yams. Then they picked up bread cubes, buns, some fudge and cookies. Moving on to the meat department they added a turkey, a ham, and bacon. Mom even insisted on a shrimp tray. In the dairy aisle they added butter, cheese, yoghurt, milk, eggs, sour cream and eggnog.

When they got to the dry goods section, it was sugar, flour, seasonings, cranberries, juice boxes, shrimp sauce, pickles, mayonnaise, mustard, chips and snacks and a case of pop.

Their carts were overflowing!

When they got to the check-out, Logan let his Mom empty her cart first. As he stood waiting to push his cart forward so she could do the same with his, he noticed a display of gift cards. One caught his eye.

"Mom, look. They have phone cards here. Instead of the father sending cards to his family, why don't we get him one of these so he can actually call them?"

"Oh, Logan, you are brilliant. That is a perfect idea."

They grabbed not one, but two phone cards and on the front of each card was a shining star.

Logan's eyes just about popped when the cashier told his Mom the total. His Mom did not even blink.

When they finally got home, Logan was so glad his Dad was there waiting for them to help unload it all.

They pulled out the bin the Church had given them and added in all the food along with the gifts his Mom had quickly wrapped. She even put in a box of her Cranberry Pistachio Bark that she made every Christmas.

Watching his Mom and Dad load it all up he thought of the little boy named Padget who needed clothes.

"Mom, would it be okay if I gave that boy my old winter coat? I really don't need it anymore and I know it gets stuck all the time because I am really too big for it."

His Mom and Dad looked at him, smiled and his Mom said, "Yes, Logan, that would be a perfect thing to give this boy. That is what Christmas is all about, Son, celebrating the birth of Christ and putting the needs of others before your own."

His Dad loaded the plastic bin and a couple of other boxes they had filled into the van and drove it to the Church.

On Christmas Eve, Logan and his parents, along with his Grandparents, Aunts, Uncles and cousins, all went to the early service at Church.

When they were waiting in line to grab their coats from the racks before heading out into the cold night air, Logan saw his old coat.

There was a little boy with a man who had a baby girl in his arms. They all looked very happy. Logan pulled on his Mom's coat sleeve and pointed the family out to her.

"Mom, that must be the family we bought for. Look! He's wearing my old coat!"

Logan's Mom whispered back, "Logan, we must not let on that it was us . . . remember we are 'Secret Santas'." Logan nodded his head in agreement and beamed when he looked back at the family.

"Mom, I like being Santa!"

The End

Cranberry Pistachio Bark

1 lb. of good quality white chocolate
1 cup dried cranberries
1 cup shelled pistachios

Melt chocolate in the top of a double boiler. Let cool to room temperature. Roast pistachios at 350 degrees for 5–7 minutes. Set aside to cool.

Stir cranberries and pistachios into melted chocolate.

Pour onto foil-lined (10x15) edged cookie sheet. Refrigerate for at least 1 hour, then break into pieces. Makes about 1½ lbs.

20. "Tradition!"

ippee was the first thought Noah had when he woke up that morning. The first day of Christmas break. He jumped out of his bed, made a quick stop in the bathroom and then headed down to the kitchen.

"Mommmm, I'm up!" he called out. As he slid to a stop next to his Mom and Dad at the kitchen table he saw that they were dressed for work as usual.

"You guys don't work today, do you?" he whined.

'Well, sport, yes, in fact, we do. Unlike you, we are not yet on Christmas holidays," his Dad informed him as he looked over the top of the newspaper at him.

"What am I supposed to do all day then?" he asked.

"You are going to go spend the day with your Great Grandma," his Mom said with a smile.

"Ah, why I can't go to Grandma's instead?"

"Your Grandma is working today too, honey. GG is the only one free to watch you today. Now, grab a bowl and have some cereal, because I don't want to be late today and I have to drop you off."

Noah went to the pantry and chose his favourite cereal along with a banana for on top. As he munched his way through his breakfast, he thought about what toys he should grab before they left.

He finished the milk in the bottom of the bowl with a loud slurp, which earned him a disapproving glance from his Mom. He got up from the table with the toys on his mind and how little time he actually had to pack them up.

"Excuse me, aren't you forgetting something, Noah?" his Mom asked.

He looked back at the table; oops, he did it again. Grabbing his bowl, spoon and empty glass he took them over to the dishwasher and placed them in it.

"Thank you," she said drily.

He raced upstairs, threw on his clothes and grabbed his backpack. *Hmmm, GG is not all that active,* so he thought he better take things that he could amuse himself with. Lego, comic books, his pack of pencil crayons and a couple of action heroes.

"Noah; ready to go?" his Mom called from downstairs.

Together they made their way out to the garage to climb into the still frosty, cold car. *This year seems much colder than last year,* he thought.

"Now, Noah, I know you will be a perfect gentleman while you are at GG's, right?"

"Sure thing, Mom."

When they got to the building where his GG's condo was, his Mom parked in the Visitor spot and then walked him inside to ring the buzzer and then ride the elevator with him to the fifth floor.

The one thing that was cool about GG's condo was that there was a pool in the building. Although, he did not remember to pack his suit today.

Entering in to the suite, GG greeted them both with hugs and kisses and then they both wished his Mom a great day at work.

When the door closed, GG turned to him and said, "Noah, let me take a good look at you. You have grown again since I last saw you."

"Yup, GG, Dad says I will soon be as tall as him."

She laughed. "Well, I think you still have a ways to go. Now, what would you like to do first today, Noah? I have a long list of things to get done today; wrapping presents, baking and finishing the laundry."

None of that sounded like much fun. "I brought my own toys, GG, so if that is okay, I will just play on my own."

"Oh, sure, if that is what you want, Noah." She shrugged her shoulders and proceeded into her kitchen. Noah dumped out his Lego on the kitchen table.

"So, tell me about school. How has the first part of Grade 1 been?"

"Okay, I guess, GG. There are some nice boys in my class that I really like to play with. I hope I get to see some of them over the holidays so we can play with all the new toys Santa is going to bring me."

"Oh, really? Have you been a good boy this year to deserve all these toys?"

"Sure have, GG."

She chuckled and said, "Well, when I was your age we were lucky if we got a piece of candy and an orange for Christmas."

"What?" Noah asked in complete disbelief. "That was it?" He could not imagine getting just one piece of candy and an orange. "When were you born, GG?"

"Oh, WAY back in 1929."

"Golly, how old does that make you?" Noah asked.

"I am 84 years young. My parents emigrated here in 1923 from Russia with two children and then once they settled in to their new country, they had five more. I was the middle child of seven," she said.

"Did all seven of you just get an orange and a piece of candy, or was that only you because you had been bad?"

She laughed at that. "No, honey, I'm afraid it was the same for all of us. In fact, I can tell you that each year only one of us got to order a new pair of shoes; the rest of us would wear the hand-me-downs from our other siblings. My Dad, you're Great Great Grandpa, would trace the lucky child's foot on a piece of brown paper and mail it off to Sears for a new pair of shoes to fit those measurements."

"Seriously?" Noah asked in complete disbelief.

As they chatted Noah had drifted over to the stool on the other side of the island to watch her. She was cutting up something that looked like white butter into a bowl of flour.

"What are you baking, GG?"

"Tarts today, Noah. Butter tarts, mincemeat and the raspberry coconut ones you like so much. Would you like to help?"

"Well, okay. I should probably help you out since you are so old," he said with what he thought was good sense.

GG rolled out the pasty and after he washed his hands and she tied on an apron around him, he used a glass to cut small little rounds. She carefully laid them in tart pans and then added mincemeat.

"What is that stuff?" he asked.

"Well, Noah, it is called mincemeat and it has been a traditional English Christmas treat for hundreds of years."

"Really? What kind of meat is in it?"

"Well, none nowadays," she laughed.

She then gave him an even smaller glass to cut smaller rounds out, which she placed very gently on top.

When they went into the oven, Noah said, "Why do you make those every year, GG?"

"Well, it is tradition in our family to have mincemeat tarts. My husband's family was English and he used to love them. We also used to always have Christmas pudding for dessert at Christmas because of his family's traditions."

"Did your family have any traditions for Christmas besides getting just a piece of candy and an orange?"

"Oh yes, Noah. There are still lots of things we bake for Christmas that came from my Mom: the Lebkuchen that your Grampy loves so much along with the butter buds, the gingersnaps and then of course, the farmer sausage we eat for our Christmas breakfast. In fact, when your Grampy was just a little boy he and his father would drive out to the town I was from on the Friday before Christmas to pick up our order of sausage from the town butcher. The sausage was only ready on Friday each week."

"Tell me more about when you were little, GG."

"Well, Noah, when I was a child Christmas was very different in a lot of ways back then. It was simpler, but still as meaningful. We would all go to Church, of course, and then while the ham or turkey cooked we would go skating on the pond, or perhaps play card games or word games. My brother was the very best at making up rhymes."

GG had him cut out more rounds for two slightly larger tart pans. Again, she laid them very carefully into the pans.

Then she made the filling but she let Noah add in a few raisins to the bottom of each tart first.

"I got this recipe from your Great Aunt Laura, so really, in the family's history, this is a relatively new one, but we all love them because they are so oohey, goohey good."

The final tart recipe was his Great Great Uncle's favourite recipe and GG said she and his Great Auntie had been making them for Uncle Don for about forty years.

She let Noah spoon in some raspberry jam in the bottom of each tart and then filled them with a mixture of egg and coconut.

When they were finally done making tarts, GG heated up some home-made chicken soup she had made for lunch. Noah was skeptical when it did not come from a can, but he tried it and liked it.

While they ate their lunch, he saw GG cross off the three tarts on her baking list.

"GG, why do you bake so much stuff at Christmas?"

"Well, Noah, I love to do this for the ones I love. It makes me happy to see them enjoy something I've made in my kitchen. Christmas is about celebrating the birth of Christ with those you love: your family. Each family has their own traditions and because they are kept up by each generation, that is what helps make it such a special time of year. One day, I am betting that your Mom will be making these same tarts for your children. Nothing is more important than respecting and honouring your parents and those before them, by keeping up these traditions. It helps us live on after we are gone."

After they were done lunch, he helped GG fold some of her towels and then they played a game of Yatzchee. It was so simple; all you needed were five dice and a pad of paper.

They spent the rest of the afternoon looking at books. GG brought out the big Atlas she had and showed him on a map where her parents had lived in Russia, where she had grown up, where his Grampy had grown up and then finally, the town they lived in now. She also brought out old photographs and showed him people whom he had never met, or would, but their traditions still lived on.

The day seemed to pass by quickly. Before he knew it, his Mom was there to pick him up and take him home. She snuck a butter tart while she waited for Noah to get his boots and parka on.

"Oh, Grandma, these are amazing as always. I wish I could get them to turn out like this."

"Mom, I can show you how to do it," Noah offered. "GG taught me how to make all of the Christmas tarts today."

His Mom and GG chuckled at that.

When they were leaving, he gave GG a huge hug and said, "GG, can we make it a new tradition that I help you make the tarts each year?"

Tearing up, she hugged him close and said, "Oh, yes, that would be so perfect, Noah."

The End

Butter Tarts

The best tarts: rich, gooey and a bit runny. Prep your pastry for 12 tarts.

<u>Filling:</u>
    1 cup brown sugar
    A chunk of butter (about the size of an egg), melted
    1 tbsp. water
    1 cup raisins
    1 egg, beaten
    1 tsp. vanilla

I microwave the raisins in about 1 cup of water to soften them. Drain well. Place the raisins in the bottom of the pastry shell. This way you can control the number of raisins in each tart and no one gets cheated.

Beat the egg, add the sugar and beat again. Add water, vanilla and melted butter. Drop mixture into tart shells until about half-full and bake in 425 degree oven for about 15 minutes.

After baking, let cool for a couple of minutes as it makes it easier to get them out of the tart tins. Enjoy!

Raspberry Coconut Tarts

One double crust pastry recipe. Roll, cut and lay in your tart tins.

Add a dollup of raspberry jam into the botton of each tart.

Mix together:
   2 eggs
   ¾ cup sugar
   1 tbsp. lemon juice
   1½ cups shredded coconut
   1 tsp. cornstarch
   ½ tsp. salt
   ¼ cup melted butter
   1 tsp. vanilla

Fill tarts with mixture. Bake at 375 degrees for about 10 minutes. Cool before removing from tart tins. A really pretty tart at Christmas as the jam bubbles up and makes them a nice red and white with the coconut.

21. "No crib for a Bed"

The wind whipped and whistled around the buildings downtown as Blair made his way from the parking lot where he parked his car to his office tower. It was 6am. While he could have had a reserved stall in his building's underground parkade, he refused to pay the extra $200.00 per month. Better to walk two blocks each day than waste $2400.00 a year!

The streets were unnaturally quiet for the Saturday morning before Christmas. Companies would still be open on Monday and probably for only half a day on Christmas Eve, but most employees were taking unused vacation days to give them a full week off.

Not at his firm, he thought proudly. He closed down his office on Christmas Eve at 3pm, only two hours prior to regular closing time. He thought that was more than ample time for them to get to their homes or family for Christmas Eve. He also did not give them Boxing Day off since it was not officially a Statutory Holiday. He knew his staff called him "Scrooge" or "Grinch" behind his back, but it was business. He paid his staff well and had just doled out annual bonus checks, so he could not fathom why they weren't satisfied with that.

Christmas had never been the same for Blair – or held any meaning for him – since his mother had walked out on his family when he was just ten years old. His Dad had never recovered from that blow and had eventually died of a broken heart.

Nowadays, he usually just went over to his brother's house for Turkey dinner on Christmas Day. They wanted him to come for the whole day, but he could not abide all the activity and noise. Best to spend the day reading or working and then just show up for dinner a couple of hours prior. He always made sure to bring two bottles of wine for Ron and his wife Nancy.

Today he was looking forward to a quiet morning without anyone else in the office so he could review the firm's year-end financials. *It has been a good year.* He smiled with a deep self-satisfaction at all they had accomplished over the past twelve months.

As he waited for the walk light, he glanced over at his tower. He thought the management company had gone overboard this year with lights. They ran up all four corners of the building with a massive star running down the front of it. The blue star must span six floors of the tower in height. *What a waste of money!* He made a mental note to write the building manager an email and tell him so.

When the light changed to green, he made his way across the street fighting the wind the whole way. He gathered his coat lapels as close to his face as he could. It was only -12C but with the wind chill, it felt much, much colder.

The front area of the office tower had a couple of brick alcoves with benches. As he passed the first one, something caught his eye. A shopping cart was pushed up to the bench and on the bench lay a homeless person. Blair stopped and looked closer. For just one moment, he thought the face looked somewhat familiar. It was an elderly woman trying to stay warm with a ratty old blanket and a piece of plastic being her only protection from the wind and cold. He could see she had no coat, just several layers of old sweaters on. On her feet, she had a scuffed up pair of old sneakers.

My God, that could be Mom. As he studied her face, he was amazed she looked so serene and peaceful. Just as he was thinking she might have died from exposure, she opened her eyes and looked at him.

The woman held his gaze for what seemed like an eternity. It felt like she was looking right into his very soul. Then she smiled at him and said, "Merry Christmas."

Her voice shook him out of his daze and feeling entirely spooked, he turned and hurried into the building with his pass key.

Once inside, he turned and looked back at her through the lobby windows. She had sat up and was stretching. He was amazed because she acted like she had just spent the night in the finest bed. She folded up her plastic and blanket and placed them in her cart.

"Good Morning, Blair."

He turned and saw Don, the night security guard walking towards him.

"Morning, Don," Blair replied in a distracted voice.

"Was that homeless woman bothering you, Blair?"

"Oh, no. I was just watching her for a moment."

"She keeps turning up here, night after night. I'm supposed to chase her off, but I don't see how she is harming anyone. I just wish I could let her into the lobby each night where it is warm, but I would definitely lose my job over that," Don said.

"Hmmm, yes, well, they are probably right about that, Don. Have a good day."

"You too, Blair. I am off now for the rest of the week. Merry Christmas!"

Blair just gave a wave in response as he walked towards the elevators.

The elevator whisked him up to the 7th floor and he unlocked the office door, turned on the lights and made his way to his corner office.

He hung up his coat, laid his briefcase on his desk and then went to make himself a pot of strong coffee.

As he waited for the coffee to drip through, he could not get that homeless woman's smile out of his mind, or the feeling that he had just experienced something profound.

What if Mom was indeed living on the street? He wished he knew where his mother was, if she was still alive even. Had she had a happy life since leaving them? Was she happy now? And most importantly, why had she left them? So many questions that he just did not, nor ever would have answers to.

A few years back, Ron had encouraged him to use his resources to hire a private investigator to search for their Mom, but nothing had turned up.

Taking his coffee back to his desk, he fired up his computer and started going through the financials that his Director of Finance had forwarded to him. The numbers just blurred.

What good is all this profit and money if I do not do something good with it?

The one firm thing that he did remember about his mother was that a few days before Christmas she had made him and his brother go through their clothes, toys and books to gather up things for Boxing Day. They had always groaned a bit and were loath to give up any toys, but she warned them that, "Santa was watching!" She had also cajoled them with the promise of baking them her Crumb Cake for dessert that night. He had loved that cake.

He sat and pondered those days of his early childhood. That simple annual act his Mom instilled in them of thinking of others first – before the mad rush of Christmas Day – were some of the happiest memories he had of her. She was so happy when they took all their boxes into the Goodwill Depot each Boxing Day. He remembered the warm feeling of satisfaction he had felt too.

Nowadays, people just thought Boxing Day was about getting great discounts at the mall. Shaking his head in disgust, he tried to go back to his reports, but something was brewing in his mind.

Boxing Day . . . disgruntled staff . . . homeless people . . .

Suddenly, Blair jumped up and pushed back his chair. "I've got it!" he said out loud.

With a clear vision in his head, he sent the following memo via email to all his staff. He knew they would read it today as that was a clear responsibility within his companies' culture; you must always be "connected".

Memorandum
To: All Staff
From: The President
Date: Saturday, 21 December
Re: Operation Santa

In the spirit of Christmas and in honour of the true meaning of Boxing Day, please note the following:

If you would like to have Boxing Day off, then gather items today and tomorrow from your homes for a special donation for the homeless.

Bring your donations to work on Monday or Tuesday. Each employee who brings in a box of items will earn a paid day off on Boxing Day.

If you would like to volunteer two hours on Boxing Day morning to help me load up and deliver the items, then you will also earn the next day off as well.

Thanks,
Blair (aka The Grinch)

Blair hit send with a huge smile on his face. He then shut down his computer and checked his watch. 8:30am, perfect! By the time he got to the mall, they would just be opening the doors. He quickly jotted down a shopping list:

- Ladies long winter parka
- Winter boots
- Thermal socks
- Sleeping bag
- Blanket
- Mittens
- Toque
- Scarf
- Prepaid phone card
- Cash

The next two days seemed to fly by. His staff had eagerly embraced "Operation Santa". Grace, his receptionist was running out of room in the kitchen to store it all so he told her to use the boardroom. The staff all seemed highly engaged in the spirit of giving and could not believe that donating a few unwanted items could be so rewarding; not only in extra personal time, but also in the deep satisfaction that comes from thinking of others first.

The office closed down right on time on Christmas Eve at 3pm. He stood at the main office doors and sent each of his staff members off for the holidays with a "Best Wishes" and a handshake. There were ten of them that had volunteered to meet him on Boxing Day to help deliver all their donations to the shelter.

At 7am on Christmas morning, Blair excitedly drove downtown with a huge wrapped box laying on the seat beside him. He had had so much fun buying all the items on his shopping list, along with wrapping paper, ribbon and a bow. He had even thrown in a box of chocolates.

Once Blair parked his car, he almost flew the two blocks to his building. There was a light snow falling and it was quite foggy. The bright blue star on his building was glowing brightly in the cold night. He was not sure, of course, that she would be there again, but as he rounded the corner and looked into the alcove, he saw her there. She was lying in the exact same position as she had been when he first saw her on Saturday morning.

Walking up to her very quietly, he gently placed the box on the top of her cart. He glanced down at her and whispered, "Merry Christmas." It was the first time he had said those words in almost thirty-two years.

As he turned to walk away, he heard her say, "Merry Christmas to you too, my Son."

He stopped dead in his tracks. His heart swelled and tears streamed down his cheeks. For years he had dreamed of hearing those words spoken to him again. It was the best Christmas gift he had ever received and it was from a complete stranger.

"Merry Christmas, Mom, wherever you are," he whispered.

The End

Mom's Crumb Cake

Rub 2 cups of flour, 1 cup of sugar and ¾ cup of butter into crumbs. Reserve 1 cup of the crumbs.

Mix the rest with:
    1 cup buttermilk
    1 tsp. soda
    1 tsp. cloves
    1 tsp. cinnamon
    1 beaten egg
    1 cup of raisins
    1 cup of currants

Pour into a 9 x 13 and sprinkle the reserve crumbs on top and bake at 350 degrees for 45 minutes.

22. "Sugar Princess"

"Happy Birthday, sweetheart," Mom whispered to six-year-old Erica as she gently ran her hand over the top of her head.

Erica groaned in response. She was definitely not a morning person, even at this young age. Her Auntie said she was the only child she had ever heard of that did not want to get up on Christmas morning, preferring to sleep until 11 a.m. every day if she could.

As for it being her birthday, she was always a little sad because it tended to get lost in the crazy, last minute preparations of Christmas. Her birthday gifts from family usually arrived on Christmas and were inevitably wrapped in Christmas paper instead of birthday paper. She could never seem to have a birthday party with her friends either as most were already well on their way to their Grandparents' homes for the holidays.

"Honey, you really need to get up now. Your Auntie is picking us up in just a couple of hours."

At that, Erica finally sat up and rubbed the sleep from her eyes.

"Good Morning, Mom," she said in a sleepy voice.

"What would my six-year-old like for her birthday breakfast?"

"Hmm, Mom, can I have French toast please?"

"Oh, good choice, Ricky. Why don't you get your housecoat on and come help me make it?"

Erica loved to spend time with her Mom in the kitchen. She put on her pink housecoat and slippers and headed downstairs with her.

Together they made French toast and Erica had two whole pieces with lots of syrup on top. Her brother and Dad were already up and out of the house on errands.

When they were finished breakfast her Mom handed her a beautifully wrapped box.

"Today is all about creating a special day just for you, Erica. Grandma bought you this as she thought you would love it for our trip to the ballet."

Erica took the box and saw that Grandma had written the tag on it to read: "Happy Sixth Birthday to my Sugar Princess".

She ripped off the paper and opened the box. Wrapped in tissue inside was a beautiful white velvet dress with a sparkling silver waistband filled with stars. Underneath the dress were new white tights and a pair of sparkling shiny black shoes.

"Oh, it's beautiful, Mom!" she cried out in delight. The dress felt so soft and it was so pretty.

"Yes, it is beautiful . . . just like you, Ricky!"

Together they went upstairs to get ready for the ballet. Erica was not sure what it was about, just that it was a special Christmas production that only played for the four days before Christmas each year. Her Auntie had bought tickets for the afternoon performance today for her Mom, her Grandma and her as a special "birthday treat".

Soon her Auntie arrived with her Grandma already in the car. They both gave her big hugs and birthday wishes.

When Erica and her Mom were buckled up in the back seat, her Auntie gave her another present.

"Open it now, Eka . . . you might enjoy it on the way to the ballet," her Auntie said. Her Auntie loved to call her "Eka Beeka Boo", which she found funny.

The gift was a pretty book called "The Nutcracker". There were little buttons along the side that played music. Her Mom helped her read the book out loud in the car as they made their way downtown to the theatre.

She learned all about the ballet that they were about to see. It was about a little girl named Clara, who received a Nutcracker doll on Christmas Eve from her Godfather, a very talented toy maker.

As they turned the pages and read the story, Erica grew more excited. This was going to be wonderful.

Once they got to the theatre they took her to a special pre-show party that the Sugar Plum Fairy hosted. She was very pretty and dressed all in pink. At the party they gave Erica a special crown to wear to the performance. Everywhere Erica looked there were little girls all dressed up in fancy dresses and tutus. She felt like all the little girls were gathered there for her birthday party.

In the lobby area they had costumes from the show on display and ballerinas standing by for special commemorative photos.

Finally, it was time to enter the theatre. Auntie showed the lady at the door their tickets and then a young man showed them to their seats. They were up high, but they could see the whole stage.

Below the stage, there were musicians getting settled. Mom explained they were members of the orchestra and they would be playing the music that the ballet dancers performed to.

The lights went down and the Maestro raised his hands. The scene on the stage was of a street just outside the front door of a house. It was winter and snow was falling. A bunch of adults and children entered into the house and then the scene changed again and they were all in a living room having a party with a Christmas tree beautifully lit up in the backdrop. The girls got boxes and inside were dolls; the boys marched around pretending they were soldiers. Soon, Clara's Godfather arrived and gave Clara's brother a wooden horse and she got a blue Nutcracker doll.

Utterly fascinated, Erica watched it all unfold. The music and costumes were beautiful and the dancers flitted about almost effortlessly.

Soon Clara fell asleep and she had a dream wherein her Nutcracker came to life to save her from mice. The audience all laughed as twelve mice chased Clara around the living room. They were children dancers dressed up as mice and they skittered here and there.

Suddenly, she and the Nutcracker were very tiny, so tiny that they fit underneath the Christmas tree. Then they had to battle the evil rat Tsar and his Cossack rats.

Once they won the battle, they went on a journey. Their first stop was to visit the Snow Tsarina who had a long robe on like Erica's new dress, all white velvet with fur and sparkles. She was led onto the stage in a sleigh with two dancers dressed as wolves.

The stage was all sparkly and magical with white snow slowly drifting down. *The Snow Tsarina seemed to float across the stage.* Erica was not sure how she was doing that because you could not see her feet as her dress was so long.

All too soon the ballet was over. As they made their way through the lobby to the parking garage she chattered about all that she had seen and twirled about with her crown sparkling as it caught the lights.

Her Aunty drove them home and Erica saw that her Dad and brother were home now too. She rushed into the house and told them all about the Nutcracker and what she had seen that day.

After she changed out of her pretty new dress, the family sat down for a meal of tacos, her favourite meal, followed by the creamy rice pudding dessert her Grandma had brought her. When her Mom had asked what kind of cake she wanted for her birthday a few days ago, she had asked for rice pudding instead. Her brother said she was nuts to not have a cake, but she did not care . . . that is what she wanted.

Before dessert she got to open her gifts and her Mom and Dad bought her a white jewelry box with little blue stars all over it. When she opened the lid, a ballerina popped up and twirled around to music. She loved it.

When her Mom tucked her into bed that night she asked, "Erica, did you enjoy your birthday?"

"Oh yes, Mom, it was the BEST birthday party ever for me!"

"With your birthday so close to Christmas, I know it has not always been as special a day as it could be for you. But I want you to know that you were, and always will be, the *very best* Christmas gift the whole family ever received."

Erica knew she was loved by everyone in her family and that itself made her feel like a true Sugar Princess. She drifted off to sleep thinking of the music from the Sugar Plum Fairy's dance and white winter castles, sparkling with snowflakes and icicles.

The End

Mom's Creamy Rice Pudding

½ cup long grain rice
3 cups milk
½ tsp. salt
1/3 cup sugar
1 tsp. vanilla
1 cup whipped cream
1 can crushed pineapple
Drained, candied cherries

Combine rice, 2½ cups of milk, salt and sugar in top of double boiler. Cook, stirring occasionally over boiling water until tender (about 1½ hours). Remove from heat. Stir in vanilla and remaining ½ cup milk. Refrigerate several hours. Fold in ½ of the whipped cream and all of the pineapple. Garnish with rest of the whipped cream and the cherries.

23. "Dashing through the Snow"

It was just two days before Christmas, but really, given the Christmas Eve activities her family had planned, Tiffany figured she had only thirty-one hours left.

Truth be told she was exhausted. All she wanted to do was sleep through it all if she could. The Christmas "spirit" was nowhere in her personal radar, at all. Tiff gave and gave and gave to others all year long and she "was done".

She had a list of things to get accomplished today and while she was not officially at work, she had to drop off financials with the Accountant and make a couple of bank deposits, first and foremost. Then there were the personal items which included grabbing some groceries because she was having fourteen people for Christmas dinner, stocking stuffers, picking up her watches from the repair store, wrapping gifts, and if all that was not enough, she was expected at a dinner party at 5pm that evening.

She grabbed her keys, her lengthy list, and then headed out to "beat the rush". When she backed her car out of the garage, there was at least a foot of new snow waiting for her.

"Great, just great!" she muttered to herself. This was just going to make traffic even worse today.

Gritting her teeth in frustration she drove as fast as she could heading into the city. Her thoughts were interrupted when her cell phone rang. It was her Dad calling.

"Hi, honey, I have the Rullepolse ready for you to pick up and deliver."

Tiff groaned. It was an annual tradition for her family to make this Scandinavian meat dish each year. They had gathered ten days ago to assemble it and it had been soaking in a brine since then. Rullepolse was a layer of lamb flank, followed by layers of thin beef and thin pork. Between each layer they packed a mixture of sliced onions with about eight spices and salt petre. The layers were then rolled together and tied with butcher's twine and placed in the brine, which was spiced as well.

Her Dad continued: "I boiled it yesterday morning, Tiff, and pressed it all day so I have the three pieces for Jack and Sharon, Bob, and Tom, cut and wrapped."

With a sigh, Tiff said, "Okay, Dad, I will be there in about an hour."

She disconnected the call and groaned.

Within the hour she had made it to the bank and the Accountant's and had swung by her Dad's house. Her Mom was baking holiday bread but had taken the time to wrap the Rullepolse in clear cello bags that had white stars all over them, tied with a silver ribbon. Tiff had to admit that they looked very festive.

Setting out again for the next round of errands, she hoped she would "catch some breaks" as she had during the first hour of her trek. A lady had let her into a different lane of solid traffic and a teller at the bank had opened up the business window when she had seen her. That had allowed her to skip the long line of people waiting to make their withdrawals or deposits.

As she got back on to the main streets, Tiff could start to smell the Rullepolse. To her, that smell was Christmas. While she was dreading making these drops, she knew that her friends really looked forward to receiving this annual gift from her family.

She usually loved visiting her friends, but she knew each of them had been through very trying times this past year and could not possibly be looking forward to Christmas.

She pulled into Jack and Sharon's driveway and smiled at all the Christmas decorations on the front porch. Sharon was the original "Mrs. Claus", however, she had been battling cancer all year. Tiff knew the doctors feared it had morphed into bone cancer and as such, Sharon had had an MRI last week. Tiff was dreading the outcome.

She took a deep breath and rang the doorbell. Jacko, as she liked to call him, opened the door with a huge grin wearing a ridiculous set of reindeer antlers on his head.

"Tiffy! Welcome, welcome! Merry Christmas to you! Is that Rullepolse I smell?"

She gave Jack a big hug and then handed him her coat. Walking into the kitchen, she found Sharon baking her famous Toffee Bars in her kitchen with Bing Crosby playing in the background.

After sharing a big hug, Sharon poured her a cup of hot coffee, which was a welcome warm up after the cold outside.

"So . . . ?" Tiff asked the dreaded question.

"All clear!" was Sharon and Jack's unified response. "So positive, the Doc is allowing us to head out on our trip south," Sharon added.

Wow! Tiff could not believe the news. *A miracle, plain and simple.*

After a quick coffee and a catch up with the couple about their Christmas plans, Tiff made it out again into the snowy conditions.

Next stop, Bob's. Again, Tiff could not imagine she would find him in great spirits as he had lost his wife a few years back and was quite lonely. Feeling a little more relaxed and upbeat now, Tiff tuned the car radio to the Christmas channel for the short drive to Bob's house.

Bob greeted her at the door with his little Grandson Charlie in his arms. Tiff could hear lots of voices coming from inside. It sounded like a party.

"Tiff, how nice to see you! Come on in. The kids just got here," Bob said with a huge grin on his face. It doubled when she handed him the Rullepolse.

Again, she stayed for just a short visit, greeting all of Bob's family. She could see that her friend was happier than she had seen him in a very long time. That put a smile on her face and she carried it out to her car as she waved goodbye to them all standing in the living room window.

Two down, one to go, then grab the groceries and home to wrap.

The drive to Tom's was longer and traffic was getting busier, but the sun had come out now. Tiff found herself singing along to the tunes on the radio.

Tom was in the middle of a six-month long break from his one and only son. Tiff knew it was killing him but there were some deep principles involved and she admired him for holding firm. Along with missing the contact with his only child, whom he had raised all alone from the time the boy was two, Tom had also lost contact with his two Grandsons as a result. Tiff thought to herself that this visit was not going to go as well as the last two stops had.

Arriving at his condo, again, she found her friend in a surprisingly upbeat mood. He was busy packing for his flight home where he was going to spend Christmas with his Mom and sister.

When she handed him the little star-covered bag, he thanked her profusely.

"Tiff, this means the world to me. At least some things will be the same as they usually are this Christmas. When you can't be with the ones you love, having traditional food and honouring family customs does make it a little bit easier."

Tiff gave her friend a huge hug and wished him all the quiet blessings the season could bring.

After her quick visit with Tom she stopped for some stocking stuffers and then picked up her watches. She got to the grocery store and was amazed at how friendly and upbeat the staff were, especially given the large number of shoppers.

Heading home finally she was stopped at a red light and out of the corner of her eye she saw a car pull up next to her. She glanced over as something red had caught her eye. The driver was dressed as Santa and he looked so good! Not your average "mall variety" Santa. He noticed her staring and gave her a wave, a wink and a smile.

Something about that wink brought a tear to Tiff's eye. Here she was attempting to play "Santa" today, when really she had set out from the house in a Scrooge mood.

As she sat at that red light, she realized that if all her friends could overlook the challenges in their lives and embrace the season's joy, who was she to complain about her lot in life when it was so much better than some of those around her?

With a newfound surge of energy she said out loud, "No more Grinch allowed, Tiff! I, and I alone, am responsible for my state of mind. I choose, here and now, to enjoy the next week wholeheartedly!"

And she did have an amazing Christmas and New Year because she chose to just take it one day at a time and to see and acknowledge all the blessings in her life, and the family and friends who loved her so very, very much.

The End

Carla's Toffee Bars

½ cup butter
½ tsp. salt
1–14oz. can of sweetened condensed milk
2 tbsp. butter or margarine
2 tsp. vanilla
½ cup sugar
1 cup flour
¼ tsp. salt.

Cream butter, sugar and ½ tsp. salt. Stir in flour. Pour into ungreased 9 x 13 pan. Bake at 350 degrees until lightly browned.

In heavy saucepan stir milk, 2 tbsp. butter and ¼ tsp. salt over low heat until the butter melts. Cook and stir for about 5 minutes over medium heat. Stir in vanilla. Spread over baked layer. Bake at 350 degrees for 12–15 minutes. While still warm, spread with fudge frosting. While warm cut into bars and remove from pan. Makes 48 pieces.

Frosting:
In small saucepan melt 1 oz. square of unsweetened chocolate and 2 tbsp. butter or margarine over low heat. Stir in 1½ cups sifted icing sugar and 1 tsp. vanilla. Blend in about 2 tbsp. hot water to make a pourable consistency.

These are amazing!

24. "Mother and Child"

Today's story is dedicated to my loving mother, Elsa.

Christmas really began with a mother and her child. As such, I can think of no better time of year to honour my Mom and all the ways she has made the Christmas season so bright for us; her four, very lucky children, her three Grandchildren and now, three Great Grandkids, too!

I remember cuddling in Mom's arms. The late night drives with Dad to take Mom to work with me snuggled in against her lamb's wool coat with the soft fur collar.

I also think of all the babies my Mom helped to bring into this world, working as a Labour and Delivery Nurse for thirty-seven years. I know that each and every one of those children who were lucky enough to be held by my Mom in those first moments of life, experienced her calm loving embrace as we were so blessed to receive it each and every day. What a wonderful way to start off your life!

So, Mom, this is a huge thank you from me to you, for all these ways in which you went above and beyond to make Christmas our most cherished season of all:

- For the belief in Santa that you instilled in us and preserved.
- For going into debt each year to ensure we had everything we dreamed of, then taking the next year to pay it all off, only to do it yet again the next Christmas . . . crazy, but we know it came from your desire to give us more than you and Dad had as kids.
- For cuddling in bed with me studying the Sears Wish book, dreaming of presents to come.

- For all the lights and tinsel you strung with care.
- For raising us to appreciate your German family traditions like the Glockenspiel.
- For keeping our childhood stockings, which we all still have today.
- For all the baking you did of our favourites, just because they were our favourites.
- For teaching me how to make your perfect pastry, although it still does not have your magic touch.
- For the lessons you taught us about integrity with innovative wrapping schemes and by giving away the Mouse Trap game to Grandpa when Stu "found it" so that we could only play with it when we went to visit them in Rosthern. Stu also thanks you for busting his brand new Zorro whip over your knee on Christmas Day when he would not listen to you . . . message was received, loud and clear!
- For the shortbread you lovingly made each Christmas Eve, ensuring Dad ate some before morning, although that probably was not a hard task!
- For always making sure the unwrapped gifts from Santa were the first ones we saw.
- For the giant gingerbread man from Traeger's Bakery left by my stocking.
- For being the first house on the block with lights on at 4, 5 or 6am on Christmas morning.
- For the Christmas oranges in the toe of our stocking as homage to your humble, but loving Christmases as a child during the Depression.
- For maintaining a traditional Christmas breakfast that is still being eaten by each of your kids and their families (the fresh baked cornbread, the farmer sausage, the blood pudding, bacon and your fluffy scrambled eggs with green onions).
- For all the special "Christmas" candy in the house: Ribbon candy, Licorice All Sorts, After Eights and of course the Pot of Gold.
- For the big wooden bowl full of nuts.
- For the incredible Santa suit you made Dad.
- For the love of family gatherings . . . how to bang out Christmas dinner for thirty with a smile and warm welcome to whomever "graced our table".
- For teaching me how to make the holiday silver "sparkle".
- For teaching me the trick of ironing the linen tablecloth while still damp.
- For teaching me how to set a table that makes your guests feel special and to be a perfect host.

- For the amazing Christmas Open Houses you and Dad had each year surrounded by friends and family.
- For all the goofy paper hats we wore from the Christmas crackers.
- For the Christmas salad with the marshmallows and cherries.
- For all the lemon or hard sauces you made to go with the Christmas puddings from Auntie Eileen.
- For the "new" desserts you tried when Auntie did not make them anymore, i.e. the famous Yule Log.
- For showing me how to get cranberry stains out of the linen tablecloths and napkins the day after.
- For all the turkey soups you made with love from the leftovers.
- For each gift you ever chose for us with your loving care and attention.
- For teaching us that Christmas is all about giving, not receiving.
- For teaching us the importance of sending thank-you cards after we received gifts from our Aunties and Uncles.
- For giving us a model of what a loving, healthy marriage was.
- For making sure nothing changed at Christmas after Dad died, which I know was not easy for you.
- For never questioning the partners we chose to be with or marry and embracing them as family with a warm welcome at Christmas.
- For all the Christmas cards you chose with care signed, "Love, Mum".

And especially,

- For the love of God and our Saviour Jesus Christ. I fondly remember the Christmas Eve services we would attend together and then the Chinese dinners afterwards.

Most of all though Mom, I thank you for all the laughs we shared and the bond of family love you created, which will continue for years to come! The magic you created for each of us allows us to still feel that child-like excitement as adults each Christmas. As we grew older we recognized just how special those Christmases were at 1802 Louise Avenue.

With all my love, forever and always,
You're Baby,
Karen
XOXOX

What do you want to thank your mother for at this most Holy time of year? Cuddle up in her arms or give her a hug and share your list with her, if you can. Even if she is not with you today, mothers are always beside us, especially today as we celebrate the story of Mary, Joseph and the birth of Christ, our Saviour. Merry Christmas Everyone!

Mom's Shortbread

2 cups flour
1 cup butter
½ cup icing sugar

Cream butter and add sugar gradually. Cream well. Sift flour 3 times and add small amounts at a time. Chill in fridge for 30 minutes. Roll into logs and wrap in wax paper. Chill until firm. Slice about ½ inch thick. Top with green and/or red cherries which are sliced in half. Bake at 300 degrees until done, light yellow (not brown). About 20–25 minutes.

CPSIA information can be obtained at www.ICGtesting.com
Printed in the USA
LVIW01n1427090915
453348LV00004BB/13